Standard Relational and Network Database Languages

E. J. Yannakoudakis and C. P. Cheng

Standard Relational and Network Database Languages

With 20 Figures

Springer-Verlag
London Berlin Heidelberg New York
Paris Tokyo

E. J. Yannakoudakis, BSc, PhD, CEng, FBCS
Postgraduate School of Computer Sciences, University of Bradford,
Bradford, West Yorkshire BD7 1DP, UK

C. P. Cheng, BSc, MSc, PhD, MBCS
Department of Mathematical Studies, Hong Kong Polytechnic,
Kowloon, Hong Kong

British Library Cataloguing in Publication Data
Yannakoudakis, E.J., *1950* -
    Standard relational and network database
    languages.
    1. Machine - readable files. Software
    I. Title II. Cheng, C.P., *1947*
    005.74

Library of Congress Cataloging-in-Publication Data
Yannakoudakis, E.J., 1950-
    Standard relational and network database languages / E.J.
    Yannakoudakis and C.P. Cheng.
        p.   cm.
    Bibliography: p.
    Includes index.

    ISBN-13: 978-1-4471-3289-9   e-ISBN-13: 978-1-4471-3287-5
    DOI: 10.1007/978-1-4471-3287-5

    1. Data base management. 2. Programming languages (Electronic
computers)   I. Cheng, C.P.   II. Title.
QA76.9.D3Y365 1988
005.74--dc 19   88-31118

© Springer-Verlag Berlin Heidelberg 1988
Softcover reprint of the hardcover 1st edition 1988

Typeset direct from disk by Fox Design, Surbiton, Surrey
Printed by The Alden Press Ltd., Osney Mead, Oxford

2128/3916-543210 (Printed on acid-free paper)

Preface

For any type of software to become standard, whether a third generation language or an integrated project support environment (IPSE), it must undergo a series of modifications and updates which are a direct result of theoretical and empirical knowledge gained in the process. The database approach to the design of general purpose information systems has undergone a series of revisions during the last twenty years which have established it as a winner in many different spheres of information processing, including expert systems and real-time control.

It is now widely recognised by academics and practitioners alike, that the use of a database management system (DBMS) as the underlying software tool for the development of information/knowledge based systems can lead to environments which are: (a) flexible, (b) efficient, (c) user-friendly, (d) free from duplication, and (e) fully controllable.

The concept of a DBMS is now mature and has produced the software necessary to design the actual database holding the data. The database languages proposed recently by the International Organisation for Standardisation (ISO) are thorough enough for the design of the necessary software compilers (i.e programs which translate the high level commands into machine language for fast execution by the computer hardware).

The ISO languages adopt two basic models of data and therefore two different sets of commands: (a) the relational, implemented via the relational database language (RDL), and (b) the network, implemented via the network database language (NDL).

RDL is based on an IBM product called structured query language (SQL), whereas NDL is an extension of the previous proposal for a simple network language by the CODASYL (Conference On DAta SYstems and Languages) committee. So, the maturity of CODASYL (originally proposed in 1971) coupled with the theoretical foundations of the relational model make RDL and NDL very good candidates for the design of database compilers.

This book describes both RDL and NDL, details the syntax of their respective commands, and gives realistic examples to illustrate their use. In this sense, it is a textbook which will be of use to both students and practitioners of the database technology. In summary, the book is intended for the student taking courses (either at undergraduate or postgraduate level) on computer science, the database administrator, the database programmer who will use the commands described to develop application programs, and finally the database analyst who collects the enterprise data and proceeds to outline the logic of each application for implementation with a database language.

The book is in three parts. Part I describes the database management system as it should be, that is, the various facilities it should offer the database administrator, the programmer and the general user. Part II describes the ISO RDL including the schema and view definition language, the module language, and the data manipulation language (otherwise known as structured query language or SQL). Part III describes the ISO NDL including the commands to create the schema and the subschema, the module language and the data manipulation language.

Acknowledgements

The specification of the two ISO database languages has been a long procedure involving hundreds of specialists from all over the world. We extend our thanks to all the people involved in this important task, particularly the members of the Database Committee of the British Standards Institute (BSI) and the members of the X3H2 Technical Committee on Databases of the American National Standards Institute (ANSI).

May 1988   E J Yannakoudakis
                                                               C P Cheng

Contents

Part I
THE DATABASE ENVIRONMENT

1 Database Management Systems

1.1 Introduction

Computer-based information systems which make use of a database management system (DBMS) evolve around the concepts of field, aggregate fields, record type, and file.

(a) *Field*: The smallest unit of data which is meaningful and can represent a real-world object (e.g SALARY, NAME, JOB-TITLE). A field can be atomic, in which case it cannot be decomposed into other subfields without losing semantic information; an example of a decomposition which may be meaningless under certain applications is the integer and the decimal parts of field SALARY. Or it can be decomposable into discrete components as is the case with field NAME, which can be split into the subfields INITIALS and SURNAME. Alternative terms for field are data item and attribute.

(b) *Aggregate field*: This is a named group of fields forming a discrete structure which represents a real-world object (e.g ADDRESS, comprising the fields STREET-NO, STREET-NAME, CITY and POST-CODE).

(c) *Record type*: A collection of fields forming an inter-record structure which constitutes a logical *entity*. An example record type called STAFF is presented in Figure 1.1, comprising the fields NAME, ADDRESS, JOB-TITLE, and the inter-link component which is used to associate each member of staff

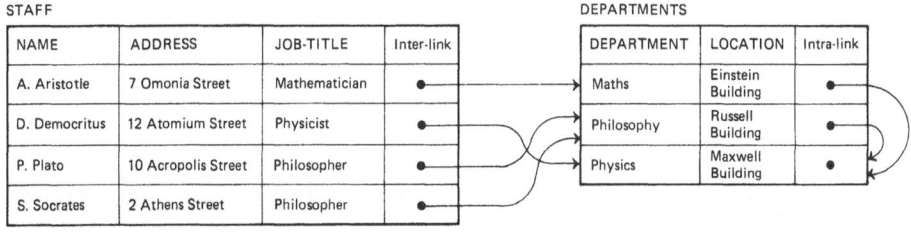

Figure 1.1 Intra- and inter-record structures.

with a department. The intra-link component of record type DEPARTMENT is used to link departments which run joint courses (a maximum of one link per record occurrence in both files STAFF and DEPARTMENT).

(d) *File*: A collection of occurrences under the same record type. The occurrence of a value under a field conforms with the specification of a single *domain* (a pre-specified set of values which can be integer, real, character, etc). Example files are presented in Figure 1.1, where a null link value signifies the end of a chain (relationship).

Clearly, the use of linked structures which are implemented on some language or other can involve one, two, or more links per record occurrence, offering alternative access paths to cluster logically related records.

Ideally, a set of files should be available for a variety of users and applications within an organisation, in such a way as to minimise redundancy (i.e duplicate record/field occurrences), while maintaining: (a) access flexibility, (b) data shareability, (c) data integrity, (d) security, and (e) performance and efficiency.

We are now in a position to define the terms *DBMS* and *database* [Yannakoudakis, 1988] as follows:

A database is a collection of well-organised records within a commonly available mass storage medium. It serves one or more applications in an optimal fashion by allowing a common and controlled approach to adding, modifying and retrieving sets of data. The DBMS is a suite of computer programs which perform these operations in a standardised and fully controllable manner.

Moreover, a DBMS offers the facility to define file control data (e.g number of fields, type of each field, number of records, etc) separate from the logic of applications, ensuring in effect *data independence*. The latter concept is of the utmost importance in a database environment and can imply:

(a) Data on the devices (e.g disks) can be manipulated independent of the logic of the applications which access it. This is referred to as *storage independence*.

(b) The view an application has of its data can be altered without affecting the stored values. This is referred to as *logical independence*.

The set of very high level commands available to both users and programmers alike, make some of the more complex conceptual operations very easy to implement under the umbrella of a DBMS. (High level commands, beyond those available in current third generation programming languages (3GL) such as Pascal, Ada, C, and COBOL, are collectively referred to as fourth generation languages (4GL).)

The comprehensive environment offered by the DBMS for the speedy development of applications regardless of the type of data they process (e.g text, numeric, graphical, image), makes it a very attractive proposition to data processing managers of today.

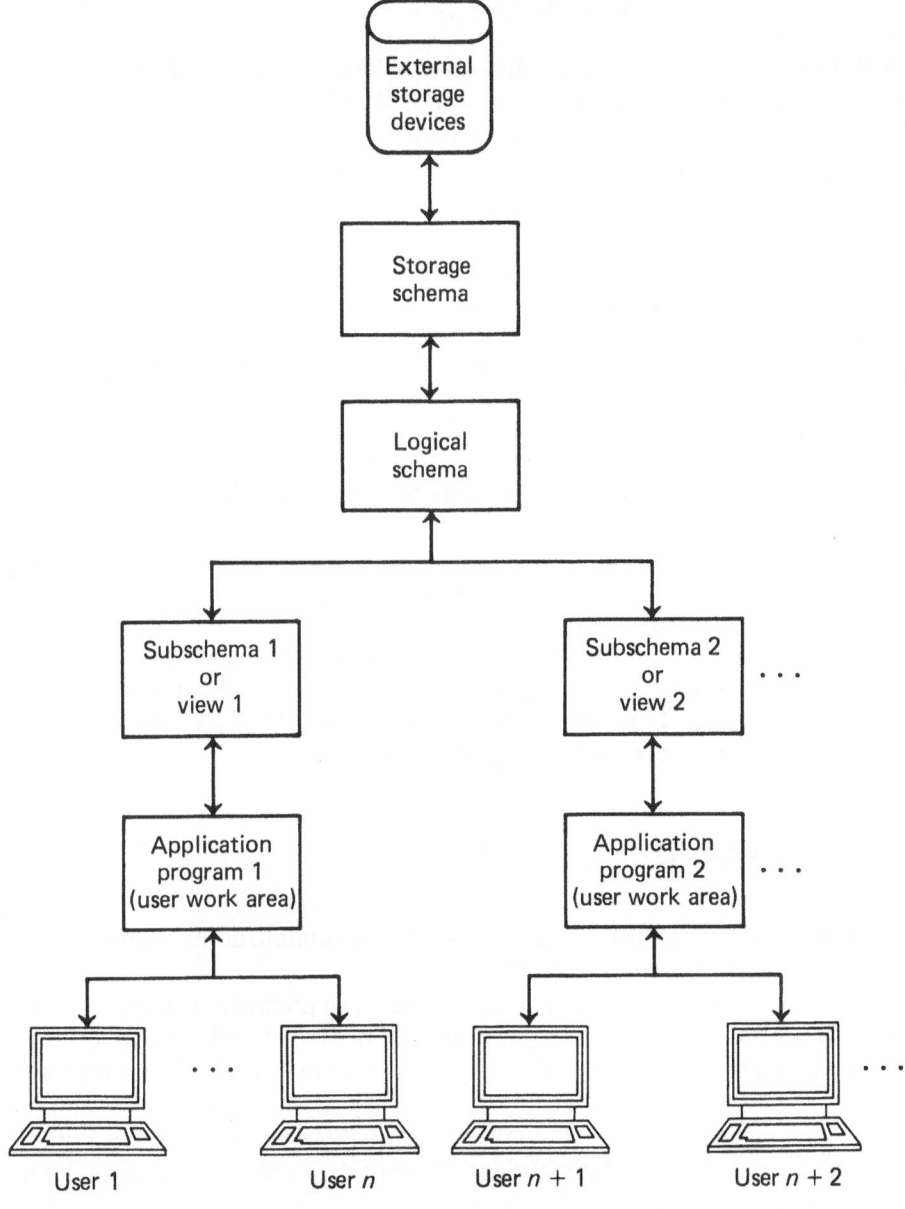

Figure 1.2   Major components of a database.

1.2 The Three Architectural Levels

With traditional file-based information systems data is stored under predefined record types which can be linked at the intra- or inter-level, that is, within and between files. The example file structure presented in Figure 1.1 illustrates both intra- and inter-fields which have to be defined explicitly within 3GLs, but not necessarily with a 4GL.

The definition of intra- and inter-links within 3GL programs is not particularly difficult, provided the complete file(s) can be stored on primary memory. If the files are too large to be held in the primary memory, then secondary memory (e.g a disk) is also used. One way of utilising both primary and secondary storage is to apply virtual storage techniques, joining in effect the available storage slots and creating a 'contiguous' block.

If virtual memory cannot be utilised, either because the operating system cannot handle it, or because the files are too large for the available virtual storage, then the definition of intra- and inter-links within 3GL programs can be problem-atic. This is due to the fact that a generalised record storage and access mechanism must be able to cope with two different types of pointers (addresses): (a) memory, and (b) secondary storage addresses.

If both storage independence and logical independence are to be maintained by the DBMS, then it must be able to cope with all possible manipulative operations upon the stored data as well as upon the views users have of it. It should also be able to cope with manipulative operations that ultimately result in the creation, deletion and updating of intra- and inter-links.

To this end, it becomes necessary to introduce a three-level architecture involv-ing: (a) the schema, (b) the subschema, and (c) the storage schema, the totality of which can maintain data independence while offering all the advantages we discussed in Section 1.1. Figure 1.2 presents an outline of this architecture which can be studied in connection with the following.

1.2.1 Logical Schema

This refers to the logical structure of the database and aims to define all the entities (record types), and their relationships.

To understand what the source logical schema can possibly contain, compare it with that portion of a 3GL program which defines the record types in terms of their name, fields, type of each field, length of each field (in bits, bytes, etc), and the way they are linked together (either explicitly or implicitly). For example, compare the logical schema with the DATA DIVISION of a COBOL program.

So, the logical schema allows the definition of data independent of the logic which manipulates it. Data formats, in general, are defined once and the fact that the schema contains the entire set of fields makes it easier to detect synonyms, homonyms and apparent definitional duplication. (Application programs which do not operate on a database must, by definition, contain a complete set of commands - possibly duplicated in other non-database programs - which describe fully each and every field they use.)

Unless otherwise stated, when we refer to a 'schema' we will imply a logical schema.

1.2.2 Logical Subschema

Given that the logical schema contains the definition of the entire database while individual applications usually require only a subset of this, it becomes necessary to specify the exact portion(s) of the logical schema which can be accessed by users and programs. The logical structure and corresponding data (including definitions and actual occurrences) of this subset is known as a *logical subschema*. (We frequently refer to this as subschema.)

So, a subschema corresponds to the view of an application and its users. If the DBMS forces each and every application program to *invoke* (reference) a subschema before it can compile successfully, then the subschema will also be introducing, to a certain extent, some form of data security since only the data (record types, field, etc) included in the subschema can actually be processed by the application program.

Clearly, in an organisation, there are as many subschemata (plural for subschema) as there are applications, although a subschema may be common to two or more different applications.

1.2.3 Storage Schema

After the logical schema has been defined the database designer considers the manipulative operations implied by the applications and proceeds to map and represent the logical schema on physical data structures which are referred to, collectively, as the *storage schema*. (Alternative equivalent terms are internal schema and physical schema.)

The storage schema comprises the definition of a set of integrated files, including flexible access paths, indexes, buffer sizes, blocking, device areas, etc which become ready (are initialised) to accept, retrieve, and generally maintain the actual values of logical schema fields.

When the database is first set up usage frequency statistics may not always be available, unless the enterprise is converting from a file-based system to a DBMS and past statistical data is available. So, the only sure way to proceed with the design of the storage schema is in an incremental and iterative manner, by collecting statistics on the usage of fields, access paths (links), etc, and subsequently using this information in order to tune the storage structures which ultimately affect the performance of the database.

1.3 Database Models

It is the type of data model and underlying data structures, which are supported by a DBMS, that will ultimately determine the viability and flexibility of accessing the various attributes of a given organisation. The types of data structures supported will also dictate the features of the data storage description language itself.

Before the database designer adopts a model or a data structure, it becomes necessary to understand data at a very much higher level - the conceptual - which is independent of logical and storage schemata. The conceptual model of an organisation is established following detailed data analyses and functional analyses, application by application. After the conceptual model has been established, the logical model can be designed by utilising only the information contained within the conceptual model.

In this sense, a *data model* represents and reflects accurately the relationships that exist among a set of record types, data items or fields. There are three major types of models where record types and their relationships may be defined as far as the logical schema is concerned [Yannakoudakis, 1988]:

(a)   Hierarchic (or tree)
(b)   Network
(c)   Relational

Each of these corresponds to a different approach to viewing an integrated set of record types at the logical schema level, irrespective of any underlying data structures at the storage schema level.

Under the hierarchic model each record occurrence has no more than one 'parent' record occurrence. Under the network model a record occurrence may have more than one 'parent' record occurrence associated with it. Under the relational model the presence of common attributes (keys) among record types forms the basis of binding record types together; here, the relationships are implicit rather than explicit as is the case with both hierarchic and network models. (The models and their corresponding languages we discuss in this book are the relational and the network.)

1.3.1 Hierarchic Model

This model can only handle one-to-one and one-to-many relationships (e.g one department many employees, many courses many departments: see Figure 1.1). The relationship many-to-one is not allowed in a hierarchy.

Generally, an element in a hierarchy can be thought of as a distinct record type which may 'own' one or more other distinct record types (the *members*). The *owner* and the *members* then form what is frequently referred to as a *set type*.

The hierarchic model binds record types together so that occurrences under a given level can be used to retrieve others directly below it. If a record occurrence is not directly below another, then it cannot be accessed directly; if direct retrieval is necessary then the occurrence is frequently duplicated under the 'parent' occurrence.

1.3.2 Network Model

This type of model allows more than one *owner* (parent) per record type. In other words, a record occurrence can be owned by two or more other record occurrences. This helps to reduce the redundancy introduced by the hierarchic model, by defining multiple incoming pointers to each record occurrence.

Although the network model allows a variable number of incoming pointers to a record occurrence, it is customary, in practice, to use the same number of 'links' per record occurrence, since variable length records are difficult to represent at the storage schema (i.e physically). While the structure is utilised and where extra links become necessary, then a tag within each occurrence may be used to indicate the presence of an overflow area which holds the rest of the links. The overflow area itself can have a fixed number of links per occurrence.

Networks sometimes give rise to *loops* or cycles where an occurrence appears to be linked to itself. This category of link occurs when a record type is defined as member and owner of the same single record type set.

If the DBMS cannot support a network model of data directly (i.e many-to-many relationships), then the network can be split into a number of one-to-many relationships which form an equivalent logical model. This becomes in effect a hierarchic model with owners and members which may be duplicated.

1.3.3 Relational Model

The relational model uses keys (primary and secondary) to form relationships among record types which are referred to as *relations*. In other words, the relationships are established through keys which are common between relations; the relationships are implicit and independent of physical implementation at the internal schema.

Each relation has associated with it a table which can be permanent and is otherwise referred to as a *base table*. The occurrences (rows) in a table are known as *tuples*. A *virtual table* is derived (synthesised) upon invocation of the corresponding virtual relation commonly known as a *view*.

The synthesis of views from one or more base tables can lead to certain difficulties when it comes to updating, inserting, or deleting occurrences in the virtual table. For example, given the following relations, based on the information presented in Figure 1.1

```
STAFF(KEY, NAME, ADDRESS, JOB_TITLE, DEPT)
DEPARTMENT(DEPT_NAME, LOCATION)
```

and the view PEOPLE which has been synthesised from attributes in relations
STAFF and DEPARTMENT

```
PEOPLE(NAME, ADDRESS, DEPT_NAME)
```

then updates on PEOPLE can result in an inconsistent database. For example, if
the insertion of a new tuple in PEOPLE contains the values:

```
J. Emmanuel, 25 Carnoustie Grove, Computing
```

then we must make sure that these values are placed at the correct underlying base
tables. Moreover, if 'Computing' is to become a new department, then it must
have associated with it a value under LOCATION. Also, the values under NAME
and ADDRESS must be assigned a unique value under attribute KEY in relation
STAFF so that the tuple can be identified uniquely.

The above considerations raise a number of axioms regarding the adoption and
usage of a relational model. The basic axioms are [Yannakoudakis, 1988]:

(a) Each table has a prespecified primary key which is capable of identifying
     tuples uniquely.

(b) Each relation has a distinct name and comprises one or more attributes.

(c) Each column of a table refers to an attribute with a name.

(d) Within a given column all entries are homogeneous (i.e they are based on a
     single domain).

(e) Duplicate tuples are not allowed.

(f) Repeating groups are not allowed.

To understand further the concept of a *repeating group*, consider the case where
department 'Maths' is housed in two buildings:

```
Maths, Einstein Building, Maxwell Building
```

In the relational model, this set of values is split between two tuples as follows:

```
Maths, Einstein Building
Maths, Maxwell Building
```

where both values (under DEPT_NAME and LOCATION) are used as a
composite primary key, conforming with axiom (a) above.

1.4 Database Languages

The adoption of the three-level architecture we discussed in Section 1.2 (i.e schema, subschema or view, and storage schema) leads naturally to the design of well-defined software modules (languages or sublanguages) which are part of the overall DBMS and enable the following tasks to be performed satisfactorily:

(a) Define the schema.

(b) Derive each subschema from the schema.

(c) Define the storage schema and initialise the underlying storage structures.

(d) Document the database environment including software, schemata, applications and users, etc.

(e) Manipulate the database directly, using high level commands (e.g a 4GL).

(f) Develop programs to satisfy peculiar application requirements by mixing commands from both a 3GL and a 4GL. (A 3GL in this case becomes a *host language*.)

What we need therefore is either a number of high level utilities as part of the DBMS, or independent (stand-alone) high level languages. In either case the objectives and tasks each set of commands performs can be defined accurately. We must not of course exclude the use of natural language for communicating with databases, although this is still in the realms of research [Yannakoudakis, 1988; Chapter 5].

1.4.1 Data Definition Language (DDL)

A DDL enables the definition of the logical schema and all subschemata. The various commands it offers enable the database designer or database administrator (DBA) to define record types, attributes, data types, and general constraints which ensure the integrity and consistency of the database.

The DDL should be for the exclusive use of the DBA, rather than the general user, since the tasks it performs are primarily definitional rather than manipulative.

1.4.2 Data Manipulation Language (DML)

As the title suggests, the DML offers a set of commands to store, retrieve and manipulate record occurrences. A DML can be a stand-alone language or it can form an extension to another high level language such as COBOL, FORTRAN, Pascal, etc (i.e a host language). A DBMS can in fact support several host languages.

The DML is primarily available for the database programmer who has knowledge of the subschema of an application and who implements the logic outlined by the database analyst.

We will avoid entering into a discussion on whether a DML is a 4GL or not because the definition, aims and objectives of a 4GL are still the subject of considerable debate and research. We do however recognise that, generally speaking, the languages or sublanguages of a DBMS form the next progressive step from 3GLs for the design of efficient, integrated and non-redundant file structures.

1.4.3 Data Storage Definition Language (DSDL)

This language provides a set of commands which aim to translate the logical schema into an internal equivalent. A DSDL is also used to manipulate and maintain the storage structures without disturbing the logical subschema in use.

A major aim of the storage schema and the DSDL is to provide a suitable environment for the collection of statistics on the usage of the database. This is necessary in order to analyse the performance of the database/DBMS and to subsequently tune it to the requirements of the users.

A DSDL is primarily available for the DBA or systems programmer and should not, under any circumstances, be accessible to the general user of a database.

1.4.4 Query Language (QL)

A QL provides a set of high level commands to interrogate the database directly; that is, without the use of a host language.

Although the QL was originally designed for the casual user, it is now widely accepted that it should be fully compatible with the DML.

The apparent deficiencies of the visual display unit (VDU) and keyboard (the most common medium for man-machine communication including the restricted page size), imply that the output from a session with a QL must be compact and neat in presentation, especially when the user is not a database expert. This, coupled with the need to keep the QL commands as simple as possible, makes it necessary for the DBMS to resort to default values regarding several items: for example, headings for values retrieved; automatic truncation of values which exceed a certain length; user-friendly responses when errors occur, etc.

1.4.5 Query By Example (QBE)

The multiplicity of attribute names and their possible codifications make it rather difficult to remember the exact 'string sequence' usually expected by both DML and QL. An alternative approach is to present on the VDU the complete set of attributes (their names and their corresponding relations) under which the user may indicate the desired cluster of values for retrieval.

To understand how the user interacts with the database through QBE, that is, through forms which are filled in by the user, consider the following example where the form (relation) STAFF contains the attributes NAME, ADDRESS and JOB_TITLE:

STAFF	NAME	ADDRESS	JOB_TITLE
	P	P	Philosopher

The letter 'P' under NAME and ADDRESS requests the QBE processor (module) to print (display) the names and addresses of all staff whose job-title is 'philosopher'.

Therefore, the use of simple commands (e.g 'P' for print, 'D' for delete, 'U' for update, and 'I' for insert), in conjunction with values under the displayed attributes, enables the inexperienced user to interrogate the database effectively.

1.4.6 Data Dictionary

The management of a database can be a very complex task and without proper documentation it is very difficult to maintain it in a consistent state. The concept of *data dictionary* fulfils part of the documentation requirements by enabling, in effect, the DBA to store on the database itself descriptive information about the database. The data dictionary can thus be classed as a *meta-database*.

The importance of data dictionaries has only recently been recognised by the database gurus and it is unfortunate that not all DBMSs provide a data dictionary module. However, this piece of software (which ideally should be fully interfaced to the database, including schema, subschemata, and storage schema), can operate in a stand-alone mode where the DBA populates it manually. That is, documentation regarding attributes and their data types, membership in record types, applications, etc can be entered by the DBA instead of being drawn from the schema and subschemata automatically.

Apart from the attributes which can be documented satisfactorily with a data dictionary processor, we can have other types of resources documented equally well. For example, we can document programs, users, complete applications, devices, etc. In this sense, the data dictionary becomes an information resource dictionary system (IRDS) [Goldfine, 1984].

On the basis of the above considerations, the IRDS can provide valuable feedback for the complete user community and generally aid the co-ordination of all database activities. Moreover, it will be able to cross-reference the entries in order to produce essential reports.

1.5 Standard Database Languages

A major milestone in the development of a DBMS was the formation of the CODASYL (Conference On DAta SYstems Languages) committee in the early 1960s. Their original objective was the extension of the COBOL language to handle files efficiently. In April 1971 the famous CODASYL proposal was published [CODASYL, 1971] which made clear the need for the three-level architecture we discussed in Section 1.2.

Since the publication of the 1971 report, we have seen various implementations of the CODASYL model, none of which could offer a complete set of languages or sublanguages to carry out the tasks of DDL, DML, DSDL, QUERY, or IRDS in an integrated manner. The problem is particularly obvious in the lack of progess on a standard DSDL, even in the current ISO proposals. (The tasks of a DSDL have always been described as 'implementor-dependent'.) Another handicap, in our view, has been the emphasis on COBOL for all database programming.

Another important development in the history of the DBMS approach to handling data was the publication of the relational model [Codd, 1970], which did not receive the attention it deserved until fairly recently.

The fact that the relational model is based on simple algebraic concepts (matrix theory in particular) has attracted the attention of numerous mathematicians and logicians who saw it as an attractive proposition to understand and explore further the world of computers. This 'jump on the bandwagon' trend gave rise to thousands of publications on relational theory with its mystifying terminology and concepts, most of which will remain in the realms of research as intellectual activities for some years to come.

In 1987 (seventeen years after the original CODASYL report), we saw the publication of two proposals for the design of database languages: one for the relational model [ISO, 1987a] and another for the network model [ISO, 1987b]. The proposals contain the formal specifications of these languages in Backus-Naur Form (BNF), written by a group of eminent scientists from all over the world. Our aim is to present these languages with examples on the use of the commands for the student and general practitioner of the database technology.

1.5.1 Notations

The syntactic notations used throughout Parts II and III in this book are explained below.

(i)   Square brackets ([ ]) denote optional elements.

(ii) Braces ({ }) group sequences of elements, of which one and only one must be chosen.

(iii) The vertical bar (|) separates alternatives from a multiple choice list of elements.

(iv) Ellipses (...) indicate elements that may be repeated one or more times. If a comma appears prior to the ellipses (,...), a comma should then be used as a separator between any two consecutive elements. For example,

```
{literal}...
```

means literal1 literal2 literal3 and so on, while

```
{literal},...
```

means literal1, literal2, literal3 and so on.

(v) Words in upper case letters and lower case letters are keywords and elements respectively. Elements are written in hyphenated words in the general format for a more precise presentation. For example, 'column name' is written as 'column-name' in the format, 'search condition' is written as 'search-condition', and so on.

1.5.2 Elementary Terms

In what follows we present the elementary terms common to both relational and network database languages [Yannakoudakis & Cheng, 1987].

Character

A character can either be a digit (0, 1, 2, ..., 9), upper case letter (A, B, C, ..., Z), lower case letter (a, b, c, ..., z) or a special character defined by the implementor.

Character string

A character string consists of a sequence of characters; the number of characters in the sequence is referred to as the length of the character string. For example, the character string BRADFORD has length 8.

Integer

An integer is either unsigned or signed. An unsigned integer is composed of a sequence of digits. A signed integer is an unsigned integer with a leading plus or minus sign, although the plus sign is often omitted. For example, 8 and -8 are an unsigned integer and a signed integer respectively.

Literal

A literal is either a character string literal or a numeric literal.

Character string literal

In SQL, a character string literal is specified by a character string which is delimited at the beginning and the end by the quote mark (e.g 'BRADFORD UNI-VERSITY'). A quote mark can appear in a character string literal but it must be written as two consecutive quote marks (e.g 'BRADFORD''S NATIONAL MUSEUM OF PHOTOGRAPHY FILM AND TELEVISION'). In NDL, the double quote mark is used in the specification of a character string literal (see Section 6.4).

Numeric literal

A numeric literal is either an exact numeric literal or an approximate numeric literal. An exact numeric literal has the format

```
[+|-] {   unsigned-integer [.unsigned-integer]
      |  unsigned-integer.
      |  .unsigned-integer
      }
```

Clearly, an integer is also an exact numeric literal.

An exact numeric literal has a precision and a scale. The precision is an unsigned integer other than the digit zero (0) that specifies the number of significant digits in the exact numeric literal. The scale is an unsigned integer that specifies the number of significant digits to the right of the decimal point.

An approximate numeric literal has the format

```
{mantissa} E {exponent}
```

where the mantissa is an exact numeric literal and the exponent is a signed integer. For example, 2.1E-2, -12.34E6, etc.

An approximate numeric literal has a precision, which is an unsigned integer other than the digit zero that specifies the number of significant digits in the mantissa.

Character string value

The value of a character string literal is the sequence of characters that it contains; this is referred to as character string value. Note that this value, i.e the sequence of characters, represents a real or abstract object in the real world. For example, '10 DOWNING STREET' represents a physical building, 'HAPPY' represents a feeling of joy and 'A1' may represent a variable in an array.

Number and numeric value

Number and numeric value are both abstractions of quantity; these two terms can be used interchangeably. Unsigned and signed integers are representations of numbers or numeric values, and it can be stated that integers have numeric values. Moreover, the exact numeric literal with the format shown above can be derived in the usual mathematical way. For example, using the mathematical formalism rather than the data type definition, the exact numeric literal +327.9 has the value

$$3 \times 10^2 + 2 \times 10^1 + 7 \times 10^0 + 9 \times 10^{-1}$$

The numeric value of an approximate numeric literal is the product of the numeric value of the mantissa and the numeric value obtained by raising 10 to the power represented by the exponent.

Since numeric value, like number, is an abstraction of quantity, it can neither be termed exact nor approximate. We may, however, use the term 'exact numeric value' to mean a number or a numeric value represented by an exact numeric literal, and the term 'approximate numeric value' to mean a number or numeric value represented by an approximate numeric literal. For example, 'The *estimated* population of London is...'. If the estimated number is represented by the literal 9000000, we call it an exact numeric value; if it is represented by the literal 9E6, we call it an approximate numeric value.

Data type

A data type is a set of representable values, which are logically represented by literals. There are three data types: character string, exact numeric, and approximate numeric. Every data item (the smallest unit of named data in a database) belongs to one of these three types, which occurs as a character string literal, an exact numeric literal or an approximate numeric literal. In SQL, however, the default value of a data item is NULL, which cannot be compared with any literal.

Part II:
STRUCTURED QUERY LANGUAGE (SQL)

2 Relational Database Language (RDL)

2.1 Introduction

Since the influential work on the relational data model by E. F. Codd [Codd, 1970], the relational approach has gained rapid popularity in database management systems [Yannakoudakis, 1988]. The relational data model is well known for its simplicity, data independence and theoretical foundation. Languages for Relational Database Management Systems (RDBMS) are actively being developed, among which one of the most prominent is the Structured Query Language (SQL) originally proposed by the IBM Corporation [IBM, 1982, 1983].

The International Organisation for Standardisation (ISO) has recently published a proposal [ISO, 1987a] that defines a standard version of SQL. The definition of SQL is presented in Backus-Naur Form (BNF) which makes it very difficult for non-computer professionals to understand. Part II of the book provides an explanatory description of this proposal, redefines the format of each SQL statement and adopts realistic examples to illustrate their use by programmers and users alike.

The schema definition language (SQL-DDL) is used to declare the structures and integrity constraints of an SQL database. Using the SQL-DDL, schemata, tables, columns, views and privileges are defined and the uniqueness constraints for tables are specified.

The module language and the data manipulation language are used to declare database procedures and executable statements respectively, for a specific database application.

One of the most important features of the ISO standard is the facility to embed SQL statements in high level programming languages. This offers in effect the means to utilise well-established structured programming techniques and the extended facilities for flow control that are available in high level programming languages. To this end, the following construct is used:

```
EXEC SQL
     SQL-statement
{ END-EXEC | ; }
```

In other words, each SQL statement that appears in a host language program must be prefixed by EXEC SQL and terminated by either END-EXEC or a colon (;). Therefore, the host language program must be preprocessed so that all SQL statements can be converted to equivalent host language statements. However, the technique whereby an application program is actually compiled is implementor-dependent. Details on how to embed SQL-DML statements in host languages (including FORTRAN, COBOL, Pascal, and PL/I) can be found in the Appendices A to F of the proposed standard [ISO, 1987a].

2.2 Elementary Terms in SQL

In what follows we describe the elementary terms used in the definition of SQL commands. A complete set of keywords/commands is presented in Appendix E.

Identifier

The general format of an identifier is

```
upper-case-letter [ [underscore] {letter | digit} ]...
```

In other words, an identifier is an upper case letter optionally followed by underscores, letters, or digits with the condition that no two underscores can be used consecutively and the trailing character must be either a letter or a digit. For example, A, C_Bc6_8bc, MOTORWAY_M1, etc are identifiers. An identifier must not consist of more than 18 characters or be identical to a keyword.

Name

The database language SQL has the following names: column name, table name, correlation name, module name, cursor name, procedure name and parameter name. All of these names are expressed in the form of an identifier, with the exception of table name which has the general format

```
[authorization-identifier.] table-identifier
```

Here, the authorization identifier and the table identifier are also expressed in the form of an identifier. The use of these names will be explained later.

The format of a variable that is embedded in an application program is totally dependent on the host language used. As is well known each programming language has its own peculiar ways of declaring and using variables. However, the format of an embedded variable name in SQL is not an integral part of the ISO standard.

Newline

A newline is an implementor-defined end-of-line indicator.

Comment

A comment line has the format

```
--[character]...newline
```

The following are example comments:

```
-- HERE COMES THE SUBROUTINE
--
-- INVENTORY CONTROL
```

Separator

A separator has the format

```
{comment | space | newline}...
```

The following are example separators:

```
-- THE FOLLOWING STATEMENTS CREATE VIEW stock1
--

-- CHECK FOR THE PRESENCE OF A VALUE UNDER pay-code
```

3 Schema Definition in SQL

3.1 Schema Definition Language

For a database to be able to support different applications it becomes necessary to describe and define a global schema which encapsulates the structural and functional requirements of an enterprise in an optimal fashion, and with minimum overlap. Understandably, different applications may have conflicting requirements and the database administrator (DBA) must ensure that these are resolved satisfactorily.

The main objective of a schema definition language is to define a schema, subschemata, and their data at the logical level, independent of any programming languages (host or otherwise), excluding any references to physical data structures or hardware features.

In the ISO standard, a schema definition language (SQL-DDL) is used to specify a schema which consists of table definitions, view definitions and privilege definitions. (A view is a named table derived from one or more tables for special user requirements. It does not exist in its own right. In the relational approach, we have no subschema although a view accomplishes more or less the same goal.) SQL-DDL performs the following tasks:

(a) Define the tables and columns and associate these with their conceptual counterparts.

(b) Specify the logical order of columns (for users' convenience).

(c) Define the data types of the columns.

(d) Impose integrity constraints (null and uniqueness) on the columns.

(e) Rename table and column names in view definition.

(f) Impose a new logical order of columns (for users' convenience) in view definition.

(g) Define new (virtual) tables by selecting columns from one or more tables.

(h) Define privileges on tables and views in order to prevent unauthorized reading or modification of columns.

As we explained in Section 1.3, in the relational model relationships between tables are established when tables share the same column(s). We may therefore say that the 'links' among tables are defined by SQL-DDL indirectly.

In SQL-DDL, a schema is defined using the format

```
CREATE SCHEMA AUTHORIZATION schema-authorization-
identifier
[   table-definition
  | view-definition
  | privilege-definition
]...
```

For example,

```
CREATE SCHEMA AUTHORIZATION ABC_COMPANY
```

The schema authorization identifier is an identifier that must be different from the schema authorization identifier of any other schema in the same DBMS environment. Tables, views, and privileges defined are considered to be owned or created by the schema authorization identifier. Facilities to destroy and modify tables, views and privileges (such as DROP TABLE, DROP VIEW, ALTER TABLE, and REVOKE) for a given schema authorization identifier are not specified in the ISO standard and are left to the implementor. (Details of a comprehensive set of commands that carry out these tasks are described elsewhere [Yannakoudakis, 1988].)

The general format of table, view and privilege definition is described in the following sections.

3.2 Table Definition

A table is defined using the format

```
CREATE TABLE table-name
({   column-name {   { CHARACTER [(length)]
                    | CHAR   [(length)]}
                | {   NUMERIC [(precision [,scale])]
                    | DECIMAL [(precision [,scale])]
                    | DEC [(precision [,scale])]
                    | INTEGER | INT | SMALLINT
                  }
                | { FLOAT[(precision)] | REAL
                    | DOUBLE PRECISION}
              }
     [ NOT NULL [UNIQUE] ]
   | {UNIQUE ({column-name},...)}...
 },... )
```

Table name

The table name has the format

```
[authorization-identifier.] table-identifier
```

When an authorization identifier is specified, it should be identical to that of the schema which contains the table identifier. For example,

```
CREATE TABLE ABC_COMPANY.EMPLOYEE
```

If the table name does not contain an authorization identifier, then it is specified implicitly as being the authorization identifier of the schema. For example, if the schema is called ABC_COMPANY, then the statement

```
CREATE TABLE EMPLOYEE
```

implies the following

```
CREATE TABLE ABC_COMPANY.EMPLOYEE
```

A named table defined by a table definition is called a base table and can be considered as an autonomous physical entity in the storage area.

Two different tables created in different schemata may have the same table identifier.

Column name

A column name is an identifier which identifies a named column.

CHARACTER [(length)]

This specifies a data type as a character string with a given length. If the length is omitted, then 1 is assumed. For example, the statement

```
ADDRESS CHARACTER (30)
```

defines the column ADDRESS as a character string of length 30.

NUMERIC [(precision [,scale])]

This specifies a data type as exact numeric with a given precision and scale. If precision is omitted, then it is implementor-defined. If scale is omitted, then zero is assumed. For example, the statement

```
GPA NUMERIC (3, 2)
```

defines the column GPA as exact numeric with precision 3 and scale 2.

DECIMAL [(precision [, scale])]

This specifies a data type as exact numeric with a given scale and with an implementor-defined precision greater than or equal to the given precision. The default values for precision and scale are the same as that of NUMERIC. The shortened form of DECIMAL is DEC. For example, the statement

```
GPA DECIMAL (4, 3)
```

defines the column GPA with implementor-defined precision greater than or equal to 4 and scale 3.

INTEGER

This specifies a data type as exact numeric, with implementor-defined precision and scale of zero. The shortened form of INTEGER is INT. For example, the statement

```
FREQUENCY INTEGER
```

defines the column FREQUENCY as exact numeric with implementor-defined precision.

SMALLINT

This specifies a data type as exact numeric, with scale zero and with an implementor-defined precision not greater than that of an INTEGER.

FLOAT [(precision)]

This specifies a data type as approximate numeric, with precision equal to or greater than the given precision. If precision is omitted, then it is implementor defined. For example, the statement

```
X FLOAT (10)
```

defines the column X as approximate numeric with precision greater than or equal to 10 (i.e the number of significant digits in the mantissa is greater than or equal to 10; see 'Numeric literal' in Section 1.5.2).

REAL

This specifies a data type as approximate numeric, with implementor-defined precision.

DOUBLE PRECISION

This specifies a data type as approximate numeric, with implementor-defined precision which is greater than that of REAL.

NOT NULL [UNIQUE]

If NOT NULL is specified, the column must contain non-null values. If UNIQUE is specified, the occurrences of the column must be unique.

UNIQUE ({column-name},...)

This specifies a uniqueness constraint for a table. Its use will be demonstrated in the following example table definition.

Let us define a table called EMPLOYEE in schema ABC_COMPANY. The table EMPLOYEE contains each employee's identity number, name, department, job, monthly salary and fringe benefits.

```
CREATE  SCHEMA AUTHORIZATION ABC_COMPANY
CREATE  TABLE EMPLOYEE
(EMP_ID   CHAR(5)  NOT NULL UNIQUE
 NAME     CHAR(20)
 DEPT     CHAR(10)
 JOB      CHAR(15)
 SALARY   NUMERIC(5)
 FRINGE   NUMERIC(5)  )
```

In the table EMPLOYEE, the value of each employee's identity number is defined to be non-null and unique. Alternatively, we may omit the keyword UNIQUE under EMP_ID and write

```
UNIQUE (EMP_ID)
```

To demonstrate further the specification of a uniqueness constraint for a table, we will take an example where no two employees can have the same name, department, and job. The statement

```
UNIQUE (NAME, DEPT, JOB)
```

implies that a complete set of values under each of these attributes must result in a unique entry in the table.

Several tables may, of course, be defined in the schema ABC_COMPANY. For example, we may define a table called MERIT, which is used to ascertain the number of employees in each department and corresponding direct costs, indirect costs, revenue and turnover.

```
CREATE  TABLE MERIT
(DEPT         CHAR(10) NOT NULL UNIQUE
 SIZE         INTEGER
 DIR_COST     NUMERIC(8)
 INDIR_COST   NUMERIC(8)
 REVENUE      NUMERIC(8)
 TURNOVER     NUMERIC(10)  )
```

3.3 View Definition

A viewed table is defined using the format

```
CREATE VIEW table-name [({column-name},...)]
AS SELECT [ALL | DISTINCT] { {value-expression},... | *}
    FROM {table-name[correlation-name]},...
    [WHERE search-condition]
    [GROUP BY { [table-name. | correlation-name.]
                column-name},...]
    [HAVING search-condition]
[WITH CHECK OPTION]
```
View definition defines a viewed table which is derived from one or more tables by the query specification SELECT-FROM-WHERE-GROUP BY-HAVING following AS. The creator (e.g DBA, programmer) of a viewed table must have permission to retrieve tuples (i.e SELECT privilege: see Section 3.4) from all the tables specified by the table names following the FROM clause. The following two sections describe the use of the query specification and the WITH CHECK OPTION.

3.3.1 Query Specification

Format:

```
SELECT [ALL | DISTINCT] { * | { value-expression },...}
FROM { table-name [correlation-name] },...
[WHERE search-condition]
[GROUP BY { [table-name. | correlation-name.]
            column-name },...]
[HAVING search-condition]
```

A query specification specifies a table derived from the result of the FROM-WHERE-GROUP BY-HAVING clauses shown above. When the asterisk (*) is specified, the result R is a table with a degree equal to the number of all the columns of the source tables specified by the table names following the first FROM clause; otherwise the degree of R is equal to the number of the value expressions following SELECT. (The format of a value expression is given in Appendix A.) In these value expressions, each column specification should unambiguously reference a column of a source table.

The query specification is used in view definition, declare cursor and insert statement, and the respective schema or module should have the SELECT privilege on the tables from which R is derived (i.e those tables specified by the first FROM clause in the query specification). The four clauses following SELECT are presented in the following sections.

(i) FROM clause

The FROM clause specifies a table derived from one or more source tables. The table name has the format [authorization-identifier.] table-identifier. (See the example in Section 3.2 under table name.) A correlation name can be used to associate a table with a particular select statement, or a query specification or a sub-query. (The description of a sub-query is presented in the following paragraph.) For example, consider the following query specification:

```
SELECT *
FROM ABC_COMPANY.EMPLOYEE EMPLOYEEX
 .
 .
 .
```

In the optional WHERE, GROUP BY, and HAVING clauses which may follow the FROM clause, the correlation name EMPLOYEEX can stand for the table name ABC_COMPANY.EMPLOYEE. (An example will be given in the paragraph that introduces the EXISTS predicate below.) In the containing FROM clause, each correlation name must be distinct and must not be the same as any table name. The same rule applies to the table name.

If only one table name is specified, the result of a FROM clause is the table identified by the table name. If two or more table names are specified, the result of the clause will be the Cartesian product of the tables identified by the table names, which is a table consisting of all possible rows r such that r is the concatenation of a row from the first table identified, a row from the second table identified, and so on. Certain rows and columns can be eliminated from the Cartesian product, however, as shown by the examples in the following sections.

(ii) WHERE clause

The WHERE clause specifies a table derived by the application of a search condition to the result R of the preceding FROM clause (which is, as mentioned in the paragraph concerning the FROM clause above, either a table identified by a table name or a Cartesian product of tables identified by two or more table names). The search condition is applied to each row of R. The result of the WHERE clause is a table of those rows of R for which the result of the search condition is true. For example, the result of

```
SELECT *
FROM    EMPLOYEE
WHERE   JOB='MANAGER'
```

is a selection of the records of all managers in the ABC Company.

The search condition in a WHERE clause is composed of predicates, and can have very complicated expressions. Its format is given in Appendix A. The predicates are explained below.

Predicates

A predicate specifies a condition that can be evaluated to give a value of 'true', 'false' or 'unknown'. There are seven predicates to specify different comparisons and the general format is as follows:

```
{  comparison-predicate | between-predicate
|  in-predicate
|  like-predicate | null-predicate
|  quantified-predicate
|  exists-predicate
}
```

The format and description of each of these seven predicates are given below. Examples are used to illustrate their features. (Details on the syntax and general rules can be found in the ISO document [ISO, 1987a]). Sub-queries are used in the comparison, IN, quantified, and EXISTS predicates. The format of a sub-query is as follows:

```
(SELECT [ALL | DISTINCT] { * | value-expression }
 FROM { table-name [correlation-name] },...
 [WHERE search-condition]
 [GROUP BY { [table-name. | correlation-name.]
             column-name },...]
 [HAVING search-condition] )
```

The function of a sub-query is to specify a set of values (which are not necessarily unique) derived from the result of the FROM_WHERE_GROUP BY_HAVING clauses.

(1) Comparison predicate

Format:

```
value-expression { = | <> | < | > | <= | >= }
{ value-expression | sub-query }
```

A comparison predicate specifies a comparison of two values. The data types of the first value expression and the second value expession (or sub-query) should be comparable. For example,

```
SELECT  EMP_ID, SALARY
FROM    EMPLOYEE
WHERE   JOB=
        (SELECT JOB
         FROM    EMPLOYEE
         WHERE   EMP_ID='00001')
```
} sub-query

} WHERE comparison predicate

The result of this predicate will be unknown if the result of one of the value expressions is NULL or the result of the sub-query is empty, since comparisons cannot be made in these cases.

(2) BETWEEN predicate

Format:

```
value-expression [NOT] BETWEEN value-expression AND
value-expression
```

A BETWEEN predicate specifies a range comparison. The data types of the three value expressions should be comparable. For example,

```
SELECT EMP_ID, SALARY + FRINGE
FROM    EMPLOYEE
WHERE   SALARY + FRINGE
        BETWEEN 1000 AND 1500
```

(3) IN predicate

Format:

```
value-expression [NOT] IN
{ sub-query | ({value-specification},...)}
```

An IN predicate specifies a quantified comparison. The data types of the first value expression and the sub-query or all value specifications in the value list should be comparable. For example,

```
SELECT DISTINCT JOB
FROM    EMPLOYEE
WHERE   JOB NOT IN ('DIRECTOR','DEP DIRECTOR','MANAGER')
```

(4) LIKE predicate

Format:

```
column-specification [NOT] LIKE pattern [ESCAPE
escape-character]
```

where pattern and escape character both have the format of a value specification.
    A LIKE predicate specifies a pattern-match comparison. The column specification must reference a character string column, represented here by x. The data type of the pattern must be a character string, represented here by y, and the data type of the escape character must be a character string of length one, represented

here by z. For a given value x referenced by the column specification, the LIKE predicate will return 'true' if x matches y.

If the ESCAPE option is not specified then the characters in y are interpreted as follows:

(a) An underscore represents an arbitrary single character.

(b) A percentage sign represents a sequence of characters of any length, which might also be of length zero.

(c) All other characters represent themselves.

For example, '%SMITH' will match all names ending in 'SMITH' regardless of their length, 'EMP%' will match 'EMPLOYEE', 'EMPTY ROOM', etc, and 'M_D_' will match 'M.D.', etc, but not 'MD'. The SQL statement

```
SELECT  JOB, EMP_ID
FROM    EMPLOYEE
WHERE   JOB LIKE '%COMP%'
```

will retrieve all the job names and employee identity numbers that contain 'COMP'.

If the ESCAPE option is used and a value for z is specified then no substring of length 1 in y can be equal to the value in z. Each substring of length 2 in y can be the value in z followed by either the value in z again, an underscore character, or the percentage sign; in each of these three cases the two-character substring represents only the second character. For example, the statement

```
SELECT  EMP_ID
FROM    EMPLOYEE
WHERE   JOB LIKE 'COMP__PROG' ESCAPE '_'
```

will retrieve all the identity numbers of those jobs that are coded as 'COMP_PROG'.

It is also possible to mix the escape character with the other two pattern matching characters (i.e underscore and percentage sign). For example, the statement

```
SELECT  JOB, EMP_ID
FROM    EMPLOYEE
WHERE   JOB LIKE 'COMP__PROG%' ESCAPE '_'
```

will retrieve all employee identity numbers where each job name starts with the string 'COMP_PROG' and is followed by any other characters. This statement can therefore retrieve the following job names:

```
COMP_PROG
COMP_PROGR
COMP_PROGRAM
COMP_PROGRAMME
COMP_PROGRAMMER
```

(5) NULL predicate

Format:

```
column-specification IS [NOT] NULL
```

A NULL predicate specifies a test for a null value. It will return 'true' if and only if the value referenced by the column specification is NULL. For example, even if an occurrence of the column SALARY is 0, the result of the predicate 'SALARY IS NULL' is false.

(6) Quantified predicate

Format:

```
value-expression { = | <> | < | > | <= | >= }
   {ALL | {SOME | ANY} } sub-query
```

A quantified predicate specifies a quantified comparison. The data types of the value expression and the sub-query should be comparable. For example,

```
SELECT  *
FROM    EMPLOYEE
WHERE   SALARY
        < ALL (SELECT  SALARY
               FROM    EMPLOYEE
               WHERE   JOB = 'ENGINEER')
```

In this example, all employees with a salary of less than the minimum salary of the engineers will be selected. If the result of the sub-query is empty (i.e if there is no post of engineer in the company), all employees will be selected. (Note: This example is for demonstration purposes only. In fact, we can avoid this complication by ascertaining the minimum salary of the engineers beforehand.)

If ALL is changed to SOME or ANY in the example above, then all employees with a salary of less than the maximum salary of the engineers will be selected. If the result of the sub-query is empty, then no employees will be selected.

(7) EXISTS predicate

Format:

```
[NOT] EXISTS sub-query
```

An EXISTS predicate specifies a test for an empty set. For example,

```
SELECT *
FROM    EMPLOYEE
WHERE   EXISTS
        (SELECT *
         FROM    MERIT
         WHERE   DEPT = EMPLOYEE.DEPT
         AND     TURNOVER > 5000000)
```

The EXISTS predicate is true if and only if the result of the sub-query is not empty. Hence in the above example, only those employees who work in a department with a turnover of over 5,000,000 are selected.

We will also give an example using NOT EXISTS and the correlation name of a table name:

```
SELECT DISTINCT JOB
FROM    EMPLOYEE EMPLOYEEX
WHERE   NOT EXISTS
        (SELECT *
         FROM    EMPLOYEE EMPLOYEEY
         WHERE   EMPLOYEEY.JOB = EMPLOYEEX.JOB
         AND     DEPT <> 'COMP')
```

In this example, all the jobs which are available only in the department COMP are selected. As regards the syntax, the table name EMPLOYEE should not be used to identify any column. For example, an error will arise if we write EMPLOYEE.JOB = EMPLOYEEX.JOB instead of EMPLOYEEY.JOB = EMPLOYEEX.JOB in the WHERE clause of the sub-query.

(Note: In the ISO document [ISO, 1987a], the EXISTS predicate does not have the option [NOT]. We assume, however, that it is merely a misprint.)

(iii) GROUP BY clause

By applying a GROUP BY clause to the result of the previously specified clause, a grouped table will be specified. For example,

```
SELECT    DEPT, JOB
FROM      EMPLOYEE
GROUP BY DEPT, JOB
```

The above statement classifies the jobs of employees within each department. The result is a grouped table which gives a list of all department/job combinations, with duplicate pairs being eliminated.

(iv) HAVING clause

A HAVING clause specifies a restriction on the grouped table resulting from the previous GROUP BY clause or FROM clause by eliminating groups not meeting the search condition following HAVING. For example,

```
SELECT    DEPT, JOB
FROM      EMPLOYEE
GROUP BY  DEPT, JOB
HAVING    MIN(SALARY) > 1000
```

In this example, only those department/job combinations for which the minimum salary is over 1,000 are selected. (For instance, consider the post of secretary in the engineering department. If the salary of every secretary in that department is over 1,000, then the resulting grouped table will consist of the tuple 'ENGINEERING, SECRETARY'.)

In most cases, the search condition of HAVING is applied to the result of the preceding GROUP BY clause. If the GROUP BY clause is not specified, it is applied to the result of the preceding FROM clause or WHERE clause, but that result should be a single group and without a grouping column.

3.3.2 With Check Option

If the WITH CHECK OPTION is specified then the insertion or update of any rows in the viewed table should not violate the 'WHERE search-condition' which defines the view, assuming that the option 'WHERE search-condition' is specified and the viewed table is updatable. (The updatability of viewed tables is discussed in Section 3.3.3.) For example, consider the viewed table HIGH_SAL of the base table EMPLOYEE which lists those employees of the ABC_COMPANY (described in Section 3.2) who have a monthly salary of 2,000 or above.

```
CREATE VIEW HIGH_SAL
AS SELECT EMP_ID, NAME, DEPT, SALARY
   FROM EMPLOYEE
   WHERE SALARY >= 2000
WITH CHECK OPTION
```

In this case, an insertion of the row

```
('00001', 'SMITH J', 'COMP', 1999)
```

to the viewed table HIGH_SAL will not be accepted since SALARY < 2000.

3.3.3 Updatability of Viewed Tables

Operations on a viewed table are converted into equivalent operations on the underlying base table(s). For example, the UPDATE operation

```
UPDATE HIGH_SAL
SET SALARY = SALARY * 1.05
WHERE DEPT = 'COMP'
```

would increase the salaries of all staff in department COMP with a salary greater than or equal to 2000 by 5% in the base table EMPLOYEE (by the definition of the view HIGH_SAL stated earlier). However, there are views that are not updatable. We demonstrate some typical examples of created viewed tables which cannot be updated, using EMPLOYEE as the base table.

Example 1

```
CREATE VIEW INCOME (EMP_ID, NAME, DEPT, JOB, SAL_FRINGE)
AS SELECT EMP_ID, NAME, DEPT, JOB, SALARY + FRINGE
   FROM    EMPLOYEE
   WHERE   SALARY + FRINGE > 1800
```

The viewed table INCOME shows the total income of all employees. It is obvious that this table can support neither the INSERT nor the UPDATE operation against the column name SAL_FRINGE.

Example 2

```
CREATE VIEW DEPT_JOB
AS SELECT DISTINCT DEPT, JOB
   FROM    EMPLOYEE
```

The viewed table DEPT_JOB gives a list of all department/job combinations, excluding duplicate pairs. Obviously, this table is not updatable since two or more employees may have the same job title in a department.

Examples 1 and 2 show only two of the simple cases where viewed tables are not updatable. The problems concerning the updatability of viewed tables can be very complicated and much work remains to be undertaken on the theory of this subject. In the ISO document [ISO, 1987a] it is stated that any viewed table is an updatable table if the query specification in its view definition is updatable; and a query specification is updatable if and only if the following conditions prevail:

(i)   DISTINCT is not specified.

(ii)   Every value expression in the select list (i.e the value expression(s) follow ing SELECT) consists of a column specification which has the form: [correlation-name.] column-name.

(iii) The FROM clause specifies one table reference only which refers to an updatable table.

(iv)   The WHERE clause does not include a sub-query.

(v)   The query specification does not include a GROUP BY clause or a HAVING clause.

The ISO standard apparently makes the problem too easy and the above conditions are by no means sufficient. In fact, a counter-example can be easily created as follows:

```
CREATE VIEW COUNTER_EG
AS SELECT NAME, DEPT, JOB, FRINGE
    FROM    EMPLOYEE
    WHERE   FRINGE > 100
```

The query specification following AS in this view definition satisfies all the conditions (i) to (v) above, but if we try to insert a new row into the viewed table, say the row

```
('SMITH J', 'COMP', 'COMP_OFF', 110)
```

the system will have to insert the corresponding row

```
(NULL, 'SMITH J', 'COMP', 'COMP_OFF', NULL, 110)
```

into the underlying base table EMPLOYEE. The operation will fail since EMP_ID is defined to be NOT NULL UNIQUE. As a matter of fact, the EMP_ID acts as a primary key, which plays an important role in the updatability of viewed tables, but SQL has no understanding of this.

It is reasonable to presume that if conditions (i) to (v) above are satisfied, there should be a high chance of creating an updatable viewed table. Conversely, even if some of the conditions (i) to (v) are violated, there should be cases where an updatable viewed table can be created. For example, an updatable view can be created by joining tables EMPLOYEE and MERIT in such a way that the resultant view violates relational database principles, as is the case with the following view which contains duplicate attributes:

```
CREATE VIEW ANOMALY
AS SELECT EMPLOYEE.*, MERIT.*
    FROM    EMPLOYEE, MERIT
    WHERE   EMPLOYEE.DEPT = MERIT.DEPT
```

A detailed discussion on the updatability of viewed tables is beyond the scope of this book and so we must rely on the few known general rules and common sense.

3.4 Privilege Definition

A privilege is defined using the format

```
GRANT {  ALL [ PRIVILEGES]
         | { SELECT | INSERT | DELETE
           | UPDATE [({column-name},...)]
         },...
       }
ON table-name
TO { PUBLIC | authorization-identifier },...
[WITH GRANT OPTION]
```

The privilege definition defines privileges which are granted to other authorization identifiers or the public. The above format allows the granting of four basic privileges which are SELECT, INSERT, DELETE and UPDATE. If the optional list of column names is omitted, then all the columns become available for updating, otherwise only the columns specified can be updated.

Let T denote the table identified by the table name and let S be a schema authorization identifier. There are two cases of privilege definition.

Case 1. T is created in S

In this case, the options for GRANT on T are determined as follows:

(i)   If T is a base table, then the grantable privileges are SELECT, INSERT, DELETE, UPDATE or a combination of these. For example, in the schema definition ABC_COMPANY described in Section 3.1, we can add the following privilege definition. (The creation of the schemata AUDIT_DEPT and ACCT_DEPT will be explained below.)

```
GRANT SELECT, INSERT, UPDATE (FRINGE)
ON EMPLOYEE
TO AUDIT_DEPT, ACCT_DEPT
WITH GRANT OPTION
```

(ii) If T is a viewed table, then it will be either non-updatable or updatable. If T is not updatable, then the only option for GRANT is SELECT, and this SELECT privilege is grantable if and only if the SELECT privilege of all tables from which T is derived is grantable. If T is updatable, then the grantable privileges are those grantable privileges of the tables from which T is derived.

For example, with those privileges granted to AUDIT_DEPT in (i) above, we can grant privileges on viewed tables to other users as follows:

```
CREATE SCHEMA AUTHORIZATION AUDIT_DEPT
CREATE VIEW INCOME (EMP_ID, NAME, DEPT, JOB, SAL_FRINGE)
AS SELECT EMP_ID, NAME, DEPT, JOB, SALARY + FRINGE
   FROM   ABC_COMPANY.EMPLOYEE
   WHERE  SALARY + FRINGE > 1800
WITH CHECK OPTION
CREATE VIEW HIGH_SAL
AS SELECT EMP_ID, NAME, DEPT, SALARY
   FROM   ABC_COMPANY.EMPLOYEE
   WHERE  SALARY >= 2000
WITH CHECK OPTION
GRANT SELECT
ON INCOME
TO JOHN
GRANT SELECT, INSERT, UPDATE(FRINGE)
ON HIGH_SAL
TO JACK, ABC_CO_WAGES
```

AUDIT_DEPT does not have the right to delegate the privileges on the viewed tables INCOME and HIGH_SAL to other users unless the privileges on the base table EMPLOYEE are granted to AUDIT_DEPT with the WITH GRANT OPTION specified (see example in (i) above). The schema ABC_COMPANY has all the privileges on EMPLOYEE since it owns this base table.

Case 2. T is not created in S

In this case, before granting privileges on T to other users, S must have been granted the same privileges on T under some schema authorization identifier with the WITH GRANT OPTION specified. For example, we can write

```
CREATE SCHEMA AUTHORIZATION ACCT_DEPT
GRANT SELECT
ON EMPLOYEE
TO PETER
```

Note that this case is very similar to Case 1(ii) above, though T is created in S in the latter case.

4 Module Language in SQL

4.1 Tasks of the Module Language

At the application level, a program can be a segment of executable code, consisting of a number of sub-programs. A single module is associated with an application program during its execution and an application program must be associated with at most one module. During execution, a program can call procedures in a module (each of which consists of an SQL statement) to perform assigned tasks.

In this chapter we show how modules and procedures can be defined and embedded in host languages, and how SQL errors can be detected. Example cases are implemented in popular host languages including COBOL, FORTRAN and Pascal.

4.2 Module Definition and Procedure Definition

Modules and procedures are defined using the format shown over the page.

```
MODULE  [module-name]
LANGUAGE {COBOL | FORTRAN | PASCAL | PLI}
AUTHORIZATION module-authorization-identifier
[ DECLARE cursor-name CURSOR
   FOR query-expression
       [ ORDER BY { {  unsigned-integer
                      | [table-name. | correlation-name.]
                         column-name
                    } [ASC | DESC]·
                 },...
     ]
]...
{ PROCEDURE procedure-name
   { parameter-name {  {   CHARACTER [(length)]
                       | CHAR [(length)] }
                   | {   NUMERIC [(precision [,scale])]
                       | DECIMAL [(precision [,scale])]
                       | DEC [(precision [,scale])]
                       | INTEGER | INT | SMALLINT
                       }
                   | {   FLOAT [(precision)] | REAL
                       | DOUBLE PRECISION
                       }
                   }
   | SQLCODE
   }...;
   {  close statement | commit statement
     | delete statement: positioned
     | delete statement: searched
     | fetch statement | insert statement | open statement
     | rollback statement | select statement
     | update statement: positioned
     | update statement: searched
   };
}...
```

The module defined has an optional module name, which is an identifier and should be different from any other module name in the same implementor-defined environment. The LANGUAGE clause specifies the language of the program which calls the procedure of the module. The module authorization identifier identifies the module and has the privileges specified for each SQL statement in the module. Cursors can be declared in a module, and a module should contain one or more procedures.

SQLCODE is a reserved SQL variable that holds a number corresponding to an error as and when it occurs. The programmer/user therefore can check the value of this variable and take remedial action if necessary. This is explained further in Section 4.4.

DECLARE CURSOR

The DECLARE CURSOR defines a cursor specified by a cursor name. It is associated with a cursor specification which is composed of a query expression (explained in Appendix A) and an optional ORDER BY clause. Using cursor specification, a set of rows which satisfy certain prescribed criteria can be preselected from one or more tables. The SELECT statement in the query expression will not be executed until the cursor is opened using the OPEN statement in SQL-DML (see Section 5.2.3). The cursor is in fact a mechanism for accessing the rows in the set one by one. For example,

```
MODULE WAGES
LANGUAGE COBOL
AUTHORIZATION ABC_CO_WAGES
DECLARE CUR1 CURSOR
FOR SELECT EMP_ID, NAME, DEPT, SALARY
    FROM    ABC_COMPANY.EMPLOYEE
    WHERE   SALARY > 1500
.
.
.
```

After cursor CUR1 has been opened, rows consisting of employee identity numbers, names, departments, salaries of those employees with a salary higher than 1500 can be retrieved one at a time into a parameter list by a FETCH statement (see FETCH statement in Section 5.2.2). For example, suppose CUR1 is positioned at a certain row, we can write

```
FETCH CUR1
INTO PEMP_ID, PNAME, PDEPT, PSALARY
```

In a module, every cursor name is unique and if there is any parameter name contained in the cursor specification (e.g a value expression following SELECT can be a parameter), it should be defined in the procedure that has an open statement which specifies the cursor name.

The table T that is produced from the SELECT statement can be a temporary viewed table or a temporary base table, as defined by the implementor. If T is updatable, the cursor is associated with the table name specified by the FROM clause. In the example above, since T is updatable, the cursor CUR1 is positioned on a row of T and also on the corresponding row of EMPLOYEE. (The updatability of a viewed table, however, is still an open area for the researcher.) If T is not updatable, the cursor is not associated with any named table. For example, when UNION is specified in a query expression it is very unlikely that T is updatable.

ORDER BY clause

The ORDER BY clause following the query expression determines the sorted order in which the selected rows are fetched. In the example of module definition above, we may append the clause

```
ORDER BY SALARY DESC, NAME ASC
```

In this case, when the rows are fetched one by one, the order will be in decreasing order of salary of employees. When two or more employees have the same salary, the order among them will be determined by the alphabetical order of their names. It is also possible to specify the column position in the ORDER BY clause instead of the column names. In the example above, we may also write

```
ORDER BY 4 DESC, 2 ASC
```

Any table created using ORDER BY is a read-only table.

PROCEDURE

A module may have one or more procedures. Each procedure has a distinct name in the module and contains only one SQL statement. Parameter names declared in a procedure must be distinct and every parameter name contained in the SQL statement must also be declared in advance. If there is a column name identical to a parameter name, the column name should also contain a table name or a correlation name.

The format for defining data types for parameters in a procedure is determined by the language of the program associated with the module which calls the procedure. In the standard proposed, the LANGUAGE clause can specify COBOL, FORTRAN, Pascal or PL/I and the data types to be specified for the procedure parameters are summarised in Table 4.1.

Table 4.1 Data types of SQL parameters

Language specified	Data type of SQLCODE parameter	Data type of parameter-name in parameter declaration
COBOL	COMPUTATIONAL PICTURE S9(PC)	CHARACTER or NUMERIC
FORTRAN	INTEGER	CHARACTER, INTEGER, REAL or DOUBLE PRECISION
Pascal	INTEGER	CHARACTER, INTEGER or REAL
PL/1	FIXED BINARY (PP)	CHARACTER, DECIMAL or FLOAT

PC = implementor-defined precision greater than or equal to 4.
PP = implementor-defined precision greater than or equal to 15.

After the SQL statement S of a procedure has been executed successfully, the SQLCODE parameter will be set to 0, or it will be set to 100 if one of the following four cases occurs.

1. S is a fetch statement for which a next row does not exist.

2. S is an insert statement for which there is no candidate row.

3. S is a select statement whose result is an empty table.

4. S is an update statement (searched) or delete statement (searched) for which there are no object rows to update or delete.

If S has not been executed successfully, then all charges made to the database by the execution of S are cancelled and the SQLCODE parameter will be set to an implementor-defined negative numeral.

4.3 Using an Embedded SQL Module

In what follows we present an example SQL module that uses COBOL as the host language to implement a simple application which regrades employees:

```
MODULE  PERSONNEL
LANGUAGE  COBOL
AUTHORIZATION ABC_CO_PER
PROCEDURE  REGRADE
     OLD_JOB   CHAR(15)
     NEW_JOB   CHAR(15)
     INCREASE  NUMERIC(5)
     SQLCODE;

     UPDATE EMPLOYEE
     SET    JOB = NEW_JOB, SALARY = SALARY + INCREASE
     WHERE  JOB = OLD_JOB;
```

The name of the above module is PERSONNEL and the host language is COBOL. The module authorization identifier ABC_CO_PER identifies the module and must have the UPDATE privilege on table EMPLOYEE. The update privilege can be granted with the following command which forms part of the schema definition (see privilege definition in Section 3.4):

```
GRANT UPDATE
ON EMPLOYEE
TO ABC_CO_PER
```

As we have already discussed in Section 4.2 a module can contain several procedures, but each procedure can contain only one SQL statement. Clearly, the concept of module is one way to incorporate SQL statements within a host language program. In the case of COBOL, the CALL statement can be used to execute the SQL statement specified in each procedure of the module. The COBOL variables have to be declared in the data division as is the case with the following:

```
 .
 .
 .
01   OLD-JOB  PIC X(15).
01   NEW-JOB  PIC X(15).
01   PAY-RISE PIC S9(5)V.
01   SQL-CODE PIC S9(4) USAGE COMPUTATIONAL.
 .
 .
 .
```

In the above example, the COBOL data types of OLD-JOB, NEW-JOB, PAY-RISE and SQL-CODE correspond to the SQL data types of OLD_JOB, NEW_JOB, INCREASE and SQLCODE respectively. (The rules of the data type specification of the parameter SQLCODE are given in Section 4.2.)

Having defined the COBOL variables required, a CALL statement can be written in the COBOL procedure division of the associated host program to execute the SQL statement of the module. For example, the following statements assign appropriate values to the variables OLD-JOB, NEW-JOB and PAY-RISE and then call the procedure REGRADE presented earlier:

```
 .
 .
 .
MOVE 'PROGRAMMER' TO OLD-JOB.
MOVE 'ANALYST' TO NEW-JOB.
MOVE 100 TO PAY-RISE.
CALL 'REGRADE' USING OLD-JOB NEW-JOB PAY-RISE SQL-CODE.
 .
 .
 .
```

When the CALL statement is executed, the associated SQL module will receive control. After the SQL procedure REGRADE has been executed, control will be returned to the COBOL host program. The value of the parameter SQLCODE will be assigned to the COBOL variable SQL-CODE. This value can, of course, be used to check the database status after the call in the COBOL host program. If there is no database error, the CALL statement will promote every programmer to analyst with an increase of 100 in salary.

To understand further the interfacing of SQL with other popular programming languages, we present the same module (PERSONNEL), accomplishing exactly the same task using the Pascal syntax. In the following module the variable INCREASE is declared as REAL in order to conform with the ISO syntax rules of the Pascal host language:

The Pascal module

```
MODULE PERSONNEL
LANGUAGE PASCAL
AUTHORIZATION ABC_CO_PER
PROCEDURE REGRADE
     OLD_JOB   CHAR(15)
     NEW_JOB   CHAR(15)
     INCREASE REAL
     SQLCODE;

     UPDATE EMPLOYEE
     SET    JOB = NEW_JOB, SALARY = SALARY + INCREASE
     WHERE  JOB = OLD_JOB;
```

Declaration of variables in Pascal

```
.
.
.
var
     OLD_JOB:   string(15);
     NEW_JOB:   string(15);
     PAYRISE:   real;
     SQL_CODE: integer;
        .
        .
        .
```

Using the module from Pascal

```
.
.
.
begin
     OLD_JOB := 'PROGRAMMER';
     NEW_JOB := 'ANALYST';
     PAYRISE := 100;
     REGRADE(OLD_JOB, NEW_JOB, PAYRISE, SQL_CODE)
end;
     .
     .
     .
```

4.4 Error Handling in Embedded SQL

One of the most important tasks of an application program is to detect errors and
take remedial action where appropriate. This is particularly necessary when SQL
statements and procedures are embedded within the high level programming
languages specified by ISO, namely, FORTRAN, COBOL, Pascal and PL/I (see
Section 2.1).

SQL provides the construct

```
WHENEVER  {condition}
          {exception-action}
```

in order to detect errors as follows:

```
WHENEVER {  SQLERROR | NOT FOUND }
         {  CONTINUE | GOTO label }
```

where 'label' is a valid address label of the host language in use. CONTINUE
simply enables the program to continue even after an error has occurred.
SQLERROR detects a general SQL error, while NOT FOUND detects the case
where a search query has not been satisfied. For example, if the host language is
FORTRAN, then the following statements will detect an SQL error and print the
corresponding error code which is held in variable SQLCOD:

```
PROGRAM Test
 .
 .

 .
EXEC SQL
WHENEVER SQLERROR GOTO 100
END-EXEC
 .
 .

 .
100 PRINT *, 'The error detected is coded as ', SQLCOD
 .
 .

 .
```

(Note that SQLCOD is written without the 'E' to conform with the FORTRAN
requirement of a maximum of 6 characters per variable name.)

5 Data Manipulation Language in SQL

5.1 Tasks of the Data Manipulation Language

The data manipulation statements in SQL are used to perform simple record storage and retrieval in an SQL database. Every procedure in a module contains a single SQL statement which will be executed when the procedure is called by the application program associated with the module. In other words, DML is interfaced to an ordinary programming language which allows further analyses and processing of data items.

In an SQL database, data items and records are logically represented in two-dimensional tables defined in the schema. In the general formats of SQL statements specified in the following sections, the term 'table name' identifies a table defined in a schema.

5.2 DML Statements and their Classification

5.2.1 Handling of Transactions

COMMIT statement

Format:

```
COMMIT WORK
```

This statement terminates the current transaction and commits (makes perma-nent) any changes that were made to the database. When a transaction terminates with a COMMIT WORK statement all cursors that were opened by it are closed. (A transaction is a sequence of operations, including database operations, that is atomic with respect to recovery and concurrency [ISO, 1987a; Yannakoudakis, 1988].) For example, the following statements insert a new tuple into the table EMPLOYEE which is described in Section 3.2:

```
INSERT INTO ABC_COMPANY.EMPLOYEE
    VALUES ('01230','GRAY J','SALES','CLERK',700,50)
COMMIT WORK
```

In this example, the employee details inserted into the database with the INSERT command are made permanent by the COMMIT WORK statement which then makes these details available to other concurrent transactions.

ROLLBACK statement

Format:

```
ROLLBACK WORK
```

This statement terminates the current transaction with rollback so that any changes made to the database by the current transaction are cancelled and any cursors that were opened by the current transaction are closed. For example,

```
UPDATE EMPLOYEE
SET   FRINGE = 100
WHERE JOB = 'TECHNICIAN'
ROLLBACK WORK
```

In this example, the fringe of all technicians is set to 100 but the actual updates are not made permanent in the database file. This may appear to be unnecessary, but it is one way to check the validity of such an operation before it is actually performed with a COMMIT WORK statement. (The assumption we make here is that if a sequence of operations is invalid, then the error detection component of SQL software will inform the user accordingly.)

However, the true power of the ROLLBACK statement is realised in conjunction with the statements WHENEVER SQLERROR or WHENEVER NOT FOUND (see Section 4.4) whereby the user/programmer can trap errors and proceed to cancel all changes made to the database. This is illustrated in the following statements embedded in FORTRAN:

```
EXEC SQL
WHENEVER SQLERROR GOTO 100
END-EXEC
 .
 .
 .
100 PRINT *, 'The error detected is coded as ', SQLCOD
EXEC SQL
ROLLBACK WORK
END-EXEC
 .
 .
 .
```

5.2.2 Location and Manipulation of Rows

DELETE statement: positioned

Format:

```
DELETE FROM table-name
WHERE CURRENT OF cursor-name
```

This statement deletes a row of a table. Let T be the table identified by the table name at which the cursor specified by the cursor name is positioned. The cursor must already be declared in the containing module (i.e the module which contains the procedure including this DELETE statement) by a DECLARE CURSOR associated with T (which means T is identified in the first FROM clause of the query expression in the DECLARE CURSOR). The containing module should have the DELETE privilege on T. For example, suppose the module WAGES (see DECLARE CURSOR in Section 4.2) has the DELETE privilege on ABC_COMPANY.EMPLOYEE and CUR1 has been opened and positioned at a specific row which is to be deleted. We can write:

```
DELETE FROM ABC_COMPANY.EMPLOYEE
WHERE CURRENT OF CUR1
```

DELETE statement: searched

Format:

```
DELETE FROM table-name
[WHERE search-condition]
```

This statement deletes rows of a table. Let T be the table identified by the table name. The containing module must have the DELETE privilege on T. If the optional WHERE clause is not specified, all rows of T are deleted. If it is specified, then the search condition is applied to each row of T to determine whether the rows should be deleted. For example,

```
DELETE FROM ABC_COMPANY.EMPLOYEE
WHERE JOB='PROGRAMMER' AND SALARY > 2000
```

In this example, all records of the employees who are programmers with a salary greater than 2,000 a month are deleted.

The search condition may also contain one or more sub-queries. For example, suppose the management of an enterprise decides to close down those non-profitable departments with a turnover of less than 100,000 (details of which can be extracted from the table MERIT created in Section 3.2) and delete the corresponding employee records. We can write

```
DELETE FROM EMPLOYEE
WHERE DEPT IN
        (SELECT DEPT
         FROM    MERIT
         WHERE   REVENUE < DIR_COST + INDIR_COST
         AND     TURNOVER < 100000)
```

Table T, however, must not be identified in any FROM clause of any sub-queries in the search condition. For example, consider the following DELETE statement which intends to delete all the records of those employees whose job is the same as the employee with a specified EMP_ID:

```
DELETE FROM EMPLOYEE
WHERE JOB =
        (SELECT JOB
         FROM    EMPLOYEE
         WHERE   EMP_ID = '00001')
```

This statement might cause problems in the deletion of rows since the row itself which sets the criteria for the search condition will be deleted.

FETCH statement

Format:

```
FETCH cursor-name
INTO {  parameter-name [indicator-parameter]
     | embedded-variable-name [indicator-variable]
     },...
```

This statement positions a cursor on the next row of a table and retrieves values from that row. It is assumed that the cursor has already been declared by a DECLARE CURSOR statement in the containing module. After the cursor is opened, the execution of the SELECT statement in the cursor specification will result in a table T (see DECLARE CURSOR in Section 4.2). Using the cursor, the FETCH statement retrieves rows of T one at a time.

The two options available within the INTO clause, namely, parameter-name [indicator-parameter], and embedded-variable-name [indicator-variable] are referred to as the 'target specification'. The option 'embedded-variable-name [indicator-variable]' will be used only when the FETCH statement is embedded in a host language (see also Section 2.2).

The number of target specifications following the INTO clause in the FETCH statement should be the same as the number of columns of T. Moreover, each target specification and its corresponding column should have the same data type except that the former can be exact numeric or approximate numeric when the latter is exact numeric. For example,

```
FETCH CUR1
INTO PEMP_ID, PNAME, PDEPT, PSALARY
```

(Refer also to the FETCH statement under DECLARE CURSOR in Section 4.2.) In the above example, PEMP_ID, PNAME and PSALARY are character strings (the data type is the same as that of EMP_ID, NAME and DEPT) and PSALARY can be either approximate numeric or exact numeric (SALARY is of data type exact numeric).

An optional indicator may be associated with a target. If the target is a parameter name, then the indicator must be declared as exact numeric with scale 0. If the target is an embedded variable name, then its data type is dependent on the host language used. If the value of a column in a fetched row associated with a target is null, then an indicator will be specified for the target and set to -1.

If the target is of data type character of which the length x is not long enough to store its corresponding value from the current row, only the leading x characters will be stored in the target and the indicator will store the length of the corresponding value. Otherwise, the indicator will be set to 0. (If the length x is too long, there will be trailing blanks in the target.) If the target is of data type exact numeric, it should be set to a representation such that it can store all the leading significant digits of the corresponding column literal of table T. If the target is of data type approximate numeric, the exact numeric literal or approximate numeric literal of the column will be assigned to the target accordingly.

If an error occurs during the assignment of a literal to a target, then the SQLCODE parameter declared in the containing procedure will be set to an implementor-defined negative number. If table T is empty or the cursor is positioned after the last row, the SQLCODE parameter will be set to 100 and no values will be assigned to the parameters.

INSERT statement

Format:

```
INSERT INTO table-name [({column-name},...)]
{  VALUES ( {  {   parameter-name
                    [indicator-parameter]
                |  embedded-variable-name
                    [indicator-variable]
                |  literal
                |  USER
               }
             |  NULL
           },...
         )
  | SELECT [ALL | DISTINCT] { * | { value-
                                      expression },...}
    FROM { table-name [correlation-name] },...
    [WHERE search-condition]
    [GROUP BY {[table-name. | correlation-name.]
               column-name},...]
    [HAVING search-condition]
}
```

This statement inserts new rows into a table. Let T denote the table identified by the table name. The containing module should have the INSERT privilege on T. If the insert column list ({column- name},...) is not specified after the table name, it implies that the list consists of all columns of T in the order shown when T was created.

The number of items in the insert value list (i.e those parameter names, literals, etc in brackets immediately following the keyword VALUES; see also the paragraph of value specification in Appendix A for further explanation) should be the same as the number of column names in the insert column list. Moreover, each item in the insert value list and its corresponding object column should have the same data type, except that the former can be approximate numeric or exact numeric when the latter is approximate numeric.

If an insert item is a character string, its length should be less than or equal to that of the corresponding object column, which can have trailing blanks when necessary. If the insert item is of data type exact numeric, the object column should be set to a representation such that all the leading significant digits of the insert item can be stored. If it is of data type approximate numeric, the literal will be assigned to the object column accordingly. Finally, if NULL is specified, the object column should allow null values.

If T is a base table, the insertion procedure will be performed in the following steps:

(a) A candidate row for T with NULL for all columns is created.

(b) For each object column in the candidate row included in the insert column list the literal is replaced by the insert literal.

(c) The candidate row is inserted in T.

For example,

```
INSERT INTO EMPLOYEE (EMP_ID, NAME, JOB)
VALUES ('01234', 'NULL', 'CLERK')
```

will result in an insertion of the row

```
('01234', NULL, NULL, 'CLERK', NULL, NULL)
```

into the base table EMPLOYEE.

If T is an updatable viewed table, the above insertion process will be performed on the base table from which T was derived. If T is derived using the WHERE search condition with the WITH CHECK OPTION specified, then the insertion of any row should not violate the view-defining WHERE condition. For example, if we refer to the view HIGH_SAL as defined in Section 3.3.2, the INSERT statement

```
INSERT INTO HIGH_SAL
VALUES ('00001', 'SMITH J', 'COMP', 2100)
```

would result in an insertion of the row

```
('00001', 'SMITH J', 'COMP', NULL, 2100, NULL)
```

into the base table EMPLOYEE, but the operation will not be successful with any row containing a salary of under 2,000.

We may also insert rows which are derived from other tables by means of the query specification SELECT-FROM-WHERE-GROUP BY-HAVING, but T should not be identified in any FROM clause of the query specification or any sub-query contained in the query specification. For example, suppose a base table TEMP is created to give a list of those departments with revenue over 300,000 or with a turnover of over 1,000,000, and the names of their managers. The information required is drawn from the tables EMPLOYEE and MERIT (see Section 3.2). The creation of the table TEMP is trivial and is left to the reader. The INSERT statement in the procedure concerned can be written as follows:

```
INSERT INTO TEMP
SELECT EMPLOYEE.DEPT, NAME, REVENUE, TURNOVER
FROM    EMPLOYEE, MERIT
WHERE   EMPLOYEE.DEPT = MERIT.DEPT
AND     JOB = 'MANAGER'
AND     (REVENUE > 300000 OR TURNOVER > 1000000)
```

If there is no department with such a revenue or turnover, the result of the query specification (i.e SELECT-FROM-WHERE in this example) is empty and no row is inserted. The value 100 will be assigned to the SQLCODE parameter if it is declared in the containing procedure.

SELECT statement

Format:

```
SELECT [ALL | DISTINCT] { * | { value-
                                expression },... }
INTO {  parameter-name [indicator-parameter]
       | embedded-variable-name [indicator-variable]
       },...
FROM { table-name [correlation-name]},...
[WHERE search-condition]
```

This statement retrieves values from a specified row of the resultant table. The containing module should have the SELECT privilege on the tables specified by the table names following FROM in the above format. The number of target specifications (already explained under the FETCH statement in this section) following INTO should be the same as the items in the select list (which is either * or a list of value expressions following SELECT). Moreover, each target specification and its corresponding select list item should have the same data type, except that the former can be exact numeric or approximate numeric when the latter is exact numeric.

The result of the query specification SELECT-FROM-WHERE should have at most one row. For example, suppose it is required to retrieve the total income of the managers of COMP department in case the departmental net profit falls below 200,000; we can write (assuming that parameters PNAME, INCOME and NET have already been declared):

```
SELECT NAME, SALARY + FRINGE, REVENUE - DIR_COST - INDIR_COST
INTO   PNAME, INCOME, NET
FROM   EMPLOYEE, MERIT
WHERE  EMPLOYEE.DEPT = MERIT.DEPT
AND    EMPLOYEE.DEPT = 'COMP'
AND    JOB = 'MANAGER'
AND    REVENUE - (DIR_COST + INDIR_COST) < 200000
```

If the net profit is 200,000 or above, the result will be an empty table and the value 100 will be assigned to the SQLCODE parameter and no values will be assigned to the parameters. If an error occurs, an implementor-defined negative value will be assigned to the SQLCODE parameter.

The use of indicator parameters and the rules on the assignment of literals from the value expressions to their corresponding parameters are the same as those described under the FETCH statement and will not be repeated here.

UPDATE statement: positioned

Format:

```
UPDATE table-name
SET {column-name = {value-expression | NULL } } ,...
WHERE CURRENT OF cursor-name
```

This statement updates a row of a table. Let T denote the table identified by the table name. The containing module should have UPDATE privilege on T and contain a DECLARE CURSOR statement which declares the cursor and is associated with T. For example, suppose the module WAGES (see DECLARE CURSOR in Section 4.2) has UPDATE privilege on ABC_COMPANY.EMPLOYEE and CUR1 has been opened and positioned at a specific row R. The update statement

```
UPDATE EMPLOYEE
SET JOB = 'MANAGER', SALARY = SALARY * 1.2,
    FRINGE = FRINGE + 300
WHERE CURRENT OF CUR1
```

will be performed as follows:

(a)   A candidate row is created which is a copy of R.

(b)   The literals of the specified object columns JOB, SALARY, FRINGE in the candidate row are replaced by the update literals.

(c)   R is replaced by the candidate row.

If T is a viewed table derived from other tables using the WHERE search condition with the WITH CHECK OPTION specified, then the update of any row should not violate the view-defining WHERE search condition. For example, suppose a cursor called CUR2 has been declared in the module WAGES associated with the view HIGH_SAL under schema AUDIT_DEPT in Section 3.4 (the DECLARE CURSOR statement is left to the reader) and the cursor is opened and positioned on a specific row. The statement

```
UPDATE HIGH_SAL
SET SALARY = 1900
WHERE CURRENT OF CUR2
```

will be rejected since it violates the view-defining condition of HIGH_SAL.

The value expression should not include any set function specification (such as COUNT(*), AVG (column specification), etc). Every value expression and its corresponding object column should have the same data type except that the former can be exact numeric or approximate numeric when the latter is approximate numeric.

If the literal delivered by a value expression is a character string, its length should be less than or equal to that of the corresponding object column, which can have trailing blanks when necessary. If the literal of the value expression is of data type exact numeric, the object column should be set to a representation such that all the leading significant digits of the literal can be stored. If it is of data type approximate numeric, it will be assigned to the corresponding column accordingly. Finally, if NULL is specified instead of a value expression, then the object column (specified in the schema) should allow null values.

UPDATE statement: searched

Format:

```
UPDATE table-name
SET { column-name = { value-expression | NULL } },...
[WHERE search-condition]
```

This statement updates rows of a table. The containing module should have an UPDATE privilege on the table T identified by the table name. If the WHERE clause is not specified, then all rows of T will be updated, otherwise the search condition is applied to each row of T to determine whether the rows should be updated. For example, suppose every salesman in the ABC_COMPANY is regraded to sales representative and gets an increase of 100 in salary. We can write

```
UPDATE EMPLOYEE
SET JOB = 'SALES_REP', SALARY = SALARY + 100
WHERE JOB = 'SALESMAN'
```

The search condition may also contain one or more sub-queries. For example, suppose only those salesmen who work in a profitable department are eligible for regrading and a pay rise. We can write

```
UPDATE EMPLOYEE
SET JOB = 'SALES_REP', SALARY = SALARY + 100
WHERE JOB = 'SALESMAN'
AND    DEPT IN
       (SELECT DEPT
       FROM   MERIT
       WHERE  REVENUE > DIR_COST + INDIR_COST)
```

In order to avoid update problems, table T (e.g EMPLOYEE in the above example) should not be identified in a FROM clause of any sub-queries in the search condition, otherwise, we may be updating a row in which the contents are used concurrently to determine whether the row should be updated. For example, the update statement

```
UPDATE EMPLOYEE
SET JOB = 'SALES_REP'
WHERE JOB =
       (SELECT JOB
       FROM   EMPLOYEE
       WHERE  EMP_ID = '00001')
```

would cause update problems since the row which sets criteria for the search condition is to be updated also.

In 'UPDATE statement: searched', the steps in update, the conditions on table T when T is a viewed table, the restriction on value expressions, and the assignment of literals delivered by a value expression to the corresponding column are exactly the same as those described under 'UPDATE statement: positioned', and will not be repeated here. In fact, the only difference between them is that the former updates rows of a table by an optional search condition while the latter updates a single row using the CURRENT OF a cursor.

5.2.3 Manipulation of Cursors

CLOSE statement

Format:

```
CLOSE cursor-name
```

This statement closes a cursor specified by the cursor name. The cursor must have already been declared in the containing module by means of a DECLARE CURSOR statement.

DECLARE CURSOR

Format:

```
DECLARE cursor-name CURSOR
FOR query expression
    [ ORDER BY { {  unsigned-integer
                  | [table-name. | correlation-name.]
                    column-name
                } [ASC | DESC]
              },...
    ]
```

This statement defines a cursor. The detail of its format and uses are described in DECLARE CURSOR under module definition in Section 4.2.

OPEN statement

Format:

```
OPEN cursor-name
```

This statement opens the cursor specified by the cursor name, which must already be declared in the containing module. Before the execution of this statement, the cursor should be in the 'closed state'. After opening, the cursor is positioned before the first row of the table created by the cursor specification of the DECLARE CURSOR. For example, immediately after the execution of

```
OPEN CUR1
```

CUR1 will be positioned before the first row of the table consisting of EMP_ID, NAME, DEPT, SALARY of those employees with a monthly salary higher than 1500 (see module WAGES under DECLARE CURSOR in Section 4.2).

Part III:
NETWORK DATABASE LANGUAGE (NDL)

6 Network Database Language (NDL)

6.1 Introduction

One of the more mature models for describing the logical structure of a database is the network data model [Yannakoudakis, 1988]. In 1978, comprehensive specifications for a data description language and a data storage description language for network database management systems were proposed by the Data Description Language Committee (DDLC) of the Conference on Data Systems Languages (CODASYL) [CODASYL, 1978] following a number of reports and revisions since the formation of DDLC in 1971 [CODASYL, 1971]. ISO is currently proposing the definition of a standard version of a network database language (NDL) based on the DDLC report. Part III of this book is intended to give an explanatory description of the ISO proposal on database language NDL [ISO, 1987b].

6.2 General Structure of NDL

The ISO standard [ISO, 1987b] specifies the syntax and semantics of three database languages: (i) schema definition language, (ii) subschema definition language, and (iii) module language and data manipulation language. Two levels are also specified: Level 2 is the complete NDL database language and Level 1 is a subset of Level 2. Part III of the book is intended as an explanatory text on Level 2.

The data storage description language specified in an early report [CODASYL, 1978], however, is not included in the current proposal. The major differences between the previous CODASYL proposal [CODASYL, 1978] and the current ISO standard are presented in Table 6.1.

6.2.1 Schema Definition Language

The schema definition language is used to declare the structures and the integrity constraints of an NDL database.

Table 6.1   Major differences between the 1978 and 1986 NDL proposals

Specification	CODASYL 1978	ISO 1986
1. **Data Description Language**	Yes	Yes
Access control lock for the schema	Yes	No
CALL procedures on the schema	Yes	No
DML interface: SELECTION, WITHIN and AREA-ID clauses	Yes	No
Access control lock on areas	Yes	No
Tuning of database performance, including conversion between schema and sub-schema, frequency of key usage, procedure result, etc	Yes	No
Resource allocation: AREA NAME, WITHIN, ANY and OWNER clauses	Yes	No
DBA tasks: CALL procedures on area, data record, member and set	Yes	No
2. **Data Storage Description Language**	Yes	No
3. **Module language**	No	Yes
4. **DML cursor disposition**	No	Yes

6.2.2 Subschema Definition Language

The subschema definition language is used to declare a user view of the database described by the schema definition language.

6.2.3 Module Language and Data Manipulation Language

The module language and the data manipulation language are used to declare the database procedures and executable statements, respectively, of a specific database application.

6.3 Remarks on NDL Terminology

In the ISO standard, the NDL terminology is well organised and rigorously used. To quote an example, let us consider the symbol S shown in the Suppliers-and-Parts database in Appendix D. In the current standard, S is in fact an identifier which denotes a record name, and in turn this record name designates a record type.

Although our presentation of NDL is compatible with the ISO report, we use a simpler terminology in our explanatory notes of the sample NDL statements. For example, instead of writing 'the record type designated by record name denoted by S', we simply write 'record type S'. To quote one more example, the term 'schema SUPPLIERS_AND_PARTS' presented in the following chapters does not mean that SUPPLIERS_AND_PARTS is a schema; it means 'the schema designated by the schema name denoted by SUPPLIERS_AND_PARTS'. We believe that these abbreviations will make the examples given in this text more reader-friendly.

6.4 Elementary Terms in NDL

The following paragraphs describe the elementary terms used in the definition of NDL commands in Part III of the book. The description of some of the terms in NDL is the same as that of SQL presented in Part II. These terms include character, character string, integer, literal, numeric literal, character string value, and number and numeric value. Character string literal and data type in NDL are in fact also defined in the same way as in SQL but with the following slight differences (for their common definition see Section 1.5.2):

(i)   In NDL a double quote mark is used to specify character string literals, rather than a single quote as in SQL. For example, "BRADFORD UNIVERSITY", "BRADFORD""S NATIONAL MUSEUM OF PHOTOGRAPHY FILM AND TELEVISION", etc.

(ii) While a column in SQL can take NULL, the occurrence of every data item in NDL must have a literal assigned.(See DEFAULT clause in Section 7.2.2, and the data manipulation statements in Section 10.3.4.)

Identifier

The general format of an identifier is

```
{ upper-case-letter [ [underscore] { letter | digit } ]...
  | ' { escape-identifier-character | " }... '
}
```

From the general format, we see that an NDL identifier has two alternatives for identifier representation. The first alternative does not allow any quote marks, and is called a regular identifier. For example, A_road, M1, etc are regular identifiers. (Note that a 'regular identifier' in NDL is the same as 'identifier' in

SQL.) The second alternative allows quote marks, and is called an escape identifier.An escape identifier character is any implementor- defined character other than the single quote mark ('). For example, 'get-a-record', 'find-''next''-record' are escape identifiers. Escape identifiers are used for procedure names (see below) when the host programming language is COBOL. An identifier must contain at most 18 characters. (The double quote used in an escape identifier also counts as a character.)

Names

In the database language NDL, we have the following names: component name, component view name, module name, parameter name, procedure name, record name, record view name, schema name, set name, set view name and subschema name. All these names are expressed in the form of an identifier. Their use will be explained in the following chapters.

Comment

Comment has the format

```
(*[ character ... ]*)
```

For example,

```
(* THIS IS A COMMENT *)
(*                    *)
```

are comments, but the sequence of characters inside should not contain the substring '*)'.For example,

```
(* THIS IS A *) COMMENT *)
```

is illegal.

Newline

A newline is an implementor-defined end-of-line indicator.

Separator

The separator has the format

```
{ comment | space | newline }...
```

For example,

```
(* THIS IS A COMMENT*)

(*                      *)
```

is a separator.

Operand

An operand specifies a value. Its format is as follows:

```
{   {   [{record-name | OWNER | MEMBER}.] component-
        name   [subscripts]
     | component-name [subscripts] [OF {record-name |
        OWNER | MEMBER}]
    }
  | {   [record-view-name.] component-view-name
        [subscripts] [CURSOR]
     | component-view-name [subscripts] [OF record-
        view-name] [CURSOR]
    }
  | parameter-name [subscripts]
  | literal
}
```

The first three alternatives shown in the format above are called component identifier, component view identifier and parameter identifier respectively. If an operand is contained in a schema, then it must not be a parameter identifier or a component view identifier. If it is contained in a module, then it must not be a component identifier.

7 Schema Definition in NDL

7.1 Schema Definition Language

The tasks of the schema and schema definition language were described in Sections 1.2 and 3.1. In an ISO NDL database, a schema definition language (NDL-DDL) is used to specify a schema which consists of record type definitions and set type definitions. The language performs similar tasks to those discussed under the SQL-DDL, with the exception that the NDL-DDL defines tree structures instead of simple relational tables.

A schema is defined using the format

```
SCHEMA schema-name
[record-type | set-type ]...
```

A schema defines the logical structure of a database. Its name should be different from the schema name of any other schema in the same environment. For example,

```
SCHEMA SUPPLIERS_AND_PARTS
```

This example is based on the 'Suppliers-and-Parts' database used in the ISO document [ISO, 1987b]. It is in fact adapted from Chapters 24 to 26 of Date [Date, 1981]. We refer to the same example to demonstrate the use of NDL commands in this book. A brief description of the database structure is also given in Appendix D.

The options record type and set type under SCHEMA are explained in the following two sections.

7.2 Record Type Definition

A record type is defined using the format

```
RECORD record-name
[  UNIQUE {   [ record-name.] component-name
              [subscripts ]
            | component-name [subscripts ]
              [OF record-name ]
          }...
 | ITEM component-name
   { CHARACTER [ length ]
     | {  FIXED precision [ scale ]
        | NUMERIC precision [ scale ]
        | INTEGER
      }
     | { FLOAT precision | REAL | DOUBLE PRECISION }
   }
   [ OCCURS { unsigned-integer }... ]
   [ DEFAULT { character-string-literal
               | numeric-literal } ]
 | CHECK condition
]...
```

The record names in a record type definition should be distinct in the containing schema, and a record type has record occurrences. For example, the statement

```
RECORD S
```

defines a record type with record name denoted by S. As shown in the sample database in Appendix D, it has five record occurrences.

It can be seen from the above format that, apart from the record name, the description of record type has three optional parts: the record uniqueness clause (the clause which starts with the keyword UNIQUE), the component type (the clause which starts with the keyword ITEM) and the record check clause (i.e CHECK condition). These are explained below with examples.

7.2.1 Record Uniqueness Clause

A record uniqueness clause specifies a uniqueness constraint for the occurrences of a record type. For example, in the Suppliers-and-Parts example, we can write

```
RECORD S
  UNIQUE SNO
```

since every supplier has a unique supplier number. We can also write

```
RECORD SP
  UNIQUE SNO PNO
```

since not more than one shipment exists for a given supplier/part combination.

The 'record name.' is used to specify to which record type the data item, specified by the component name, belongs. This is particularly helpful when there are several data items appearing in different record types which have the same component name.

The subscripts will be used when the component name designates an array. The general format is ({operand}...), and the most common format is ({literal}...), where the literals are unsigned integers with a numeric value greater than zero. The number of literals should be equal to the number of unsigned integers in the 'occurs clause' (see Section 7.2.2) of the same component name in the same record type. For example, the clause

```
UNIQUE YEAR_MONTH(2 10)
```

specifies that the occurrences of the data item YEAR_MONTH(2 10) in the component name YEAR_MONTH are unique. (The component name YEAR_MONTH is an array, which will be explained in the occurs clause below.)

7.2.2 Component Type

In defining a component type, the component name specified following the keyword ITEM must be unique in the containing record type. Its data type must also be specified, which is either character string type, exact numeric type or approximate numeric type, as shown by the previous format.

In NDL, the use of CHARACTER, NUMERIC, INTEGER, FLOAT, REAL and DOUBLE PRECISION is defined in the same way as in SQL (see Section 3.2), with the exception that CHARACTER, NUMERIC and FLOAT have slightly different formats. (FIXED specifies an exact numeric data type with a scale equal to the specified scale and a precision greater than or equal to the specified precision.) For example, the SQL statements

```
ADDRESS  CHARACTER(30)
QUANTITY NUMERIC(5)
RATE FLOAT(10)
```

are written in NDL as

```
ITEM ADDRESS CHARACTER 30
ITEM QUANTITY NUMERIC 5
ITEM RATE FLOAT 10
```

The component type definition has two optional clauses: the occurs clause and the default clause.

Occurs clause

An occurs clause defines an array and its corresponding sizes each denoted by an unsigned non-zero integer. For example, consider a component name called YEAR_MONTH, which denotes the 120 months in the years 1977 to 1986. It can be defined within a record as

```
ITEM YEAR_MONTH INTEGER
   OCCURS 10 12
```

And so

```
YEAR_MONTH 2 10
```

denotes October 1978.

Default clause

A default clause specifies a default value for a component type. The data type of the literal specified in the default clause should conform with the component type, which will be explained as follows.

If CHARACTER is specified as the data type for the component type, the default literal should be a character string literal with length less than or equal to the length specified in the data type. For example, we may write

```
ITEM SNAME CHARACTER 20 DEFAULT "NOT AVAILABLE"
```

In this example, the default character string literal has a length of 13, and will be extended to the right with seven space characters before being assigned to SNAME.

If FIXED, NUMERIC or INTEGER is specified, the default literal must be an exact numeric literal, of which the number of significant digits to the right of the decimal point should not be greater than the scale of the data type, and the number of significant digits to the left of the decimal point should not be greater than P-S, where P and S are the precision and scale respectively specified in the data type.

If FLOAT, REAL or DOUBLE PRECISION is specified, the default literal must be an approximate numeric literal or an exact numeric literal, of which the number of significant digits must not be greater than the precision of the data type.

7.2.3 Record Check Clause

A record check clause specifies a validity condition for occurrences of a record type. For example, in the Suppliers-and-Parts example we can write

```
ITEM QTY NUMERIC 5
CHECK QTY >= 0
```

to ensure that the occurrences of data item QTY are not negative numeric literals.

The expression of a condition may be very complicated, and is explained separately in Appendix B.

7.3 Set Type Definition

A set type is defined using the format


```
SET set-name
    OWNER { record-name | SYSTEM }
    ORDER {  FIRST | LAST | NEXT | PRIOR | DEFAULT
            | SORTED { RECORD TYPE { record-name }...
                      | DUPLICATES { PROHIBITED |
                                     FIRST | LAST |
                                     DEFAULT }
                     }
          }
  { MEMBER record-name
    INSERTION { AUTOMATIC | MANUAL |
                STRUCTURAL structural-specification }
    RETENTION { FIXED | MANDATORY | OPTIONAL }
    [ UNIQUE {   [{ record-name | OWNER | MEMBER }.]
                 component-name [subscripts]
               | component-name [subscripts] [OF
                 {record-name | OWNER | MEMBER } ]
              }...
    ]...
    [ KEY {   { ASCENDING | DESCENDING }
              {   {   [{ record-name | OWNER | MEMBER }.]
                  component-name [subscripts]
                | component-name [subscripts] [OF
                    { record-name | OWNER | MEMBER } ]
              }
            | RECORD TYPE
          }...
        }...
      [ DUPLICATES { PROHIBITED | FIRST | LAST |
        DEFAULT } ]
    ]
    [ { CHECK condition }... ]
  }...
```

The set name in a set type definition must be unique in the containing schema. The owner, order and member clauses are described in the following sections.

7.3.1 Owner Clause

An owner clause specifies the owner of a set type. For example, in the Suppliers-and-Parts example, the owners of the set types SYSTEM_S and S_SP are the record types SYSTEM and S respectively.

SYSTEM is a special record type, which is assumed to have exactly one imaginary record occurrence, called the system record. Any set type having SYSTEM as its owner is called a singular set type. For example, SYSTEM_S is a singular set type and we can write

```
SET SYSTEM_S
   OWNER SYSTEM
   ORDER SORTED DUPLICATES PROHIBITED
   MEMBER S

       .
       .
       .
```

If a record name is specified, then it must designate a record type already defined in the containing schema. For example, we can write

```
SET S_SP
OWNER S
```

provided S has already been defined in a record type definition.

7.3.2 Order Clause

A set type has zero, one, or more sets in a database. An order clause specifies the ordering of member records in a set. A set consists of an owner record and zero, one, or more member records, and may intuitively be depicted as a chain of zero, one, or more pointers. For example, let us refer to the sample data of Suppliers-and-Parts database given in Appendix D. Let the five record occurrences in S be denoted by R-S1, R-S2, ..., R-S5, and the twelve record occurrences in SP by R-SP1, R-SP2, ..., R-SP12. Set type S_SP has five occurrences of sets, which are denoted by S_SP1, S_SP2, ..., S_SP5. The record occurrences in SP are ordered by the part number PNO within each S_SP occurrence, and the five sets in S_SP are depicted in Figure 7.1.

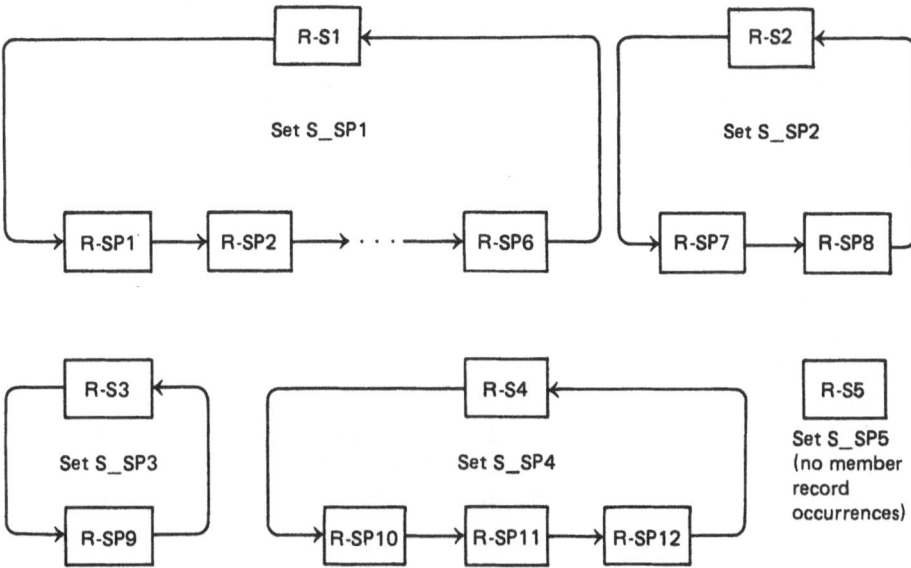

Figure 7.1   Occurrences of set type S_SP.

In the above example, we see that some prescribed ordering is assumed among the member records of sets S_SP1, S_SP2 and S_SP4. In an ORDER clause, we may have six order options for the ordering of member records in a set: FIRST, LAST, NEXT, PRIOR, DEFAULT and SORTED, which will be explained in the following paragraphs.

FIRST and LAST

If the order option is FIRST or LAST, then each incoming member record occurrence will be inserted at the first or last position of the list of member record occurrences of the set respectively. For example, if an incoming member record occurrence R-SP99 is to be inserted into set S_SP2, the results for ORDER FIRST and ORDER LAST will appear as shown in Figures 7.2a and 7.2b respectively.

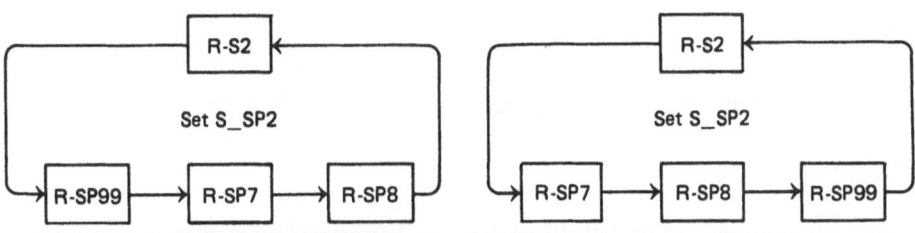

Figure 7.2a   An example of ORDER FIRST.   **Figure 7.2b**   An example of ORDER LAST.

Part of the schema description of set S_SP with option FIRST can be written

```
SET S_SP
  OWNER S
  ORDER FIRST
  MEMBER SP
```

A complete schema description for the Suppliers-and-Parts example will be given in Section 7.4.

NEXT and PRIOR

If the order option is NEXT or PRIOR, then each incoming member record occurrence will be inserted immediately after or before the latest accessed member record occurrence of the set respectively. For example, suppose the cursor is currently positioned at R-SP11 of set S_SP4.If an incoming member record occurrence R-SP99 is to be inserted, the results for ORDER NEXT and ORDER PRIOR will appear as shown in Figures 7.3a and 7.3b respectively.

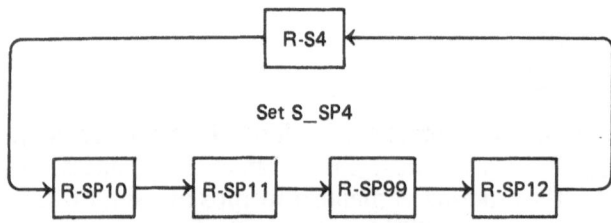

Figure 7.3a   An example of ORDER NEXT.

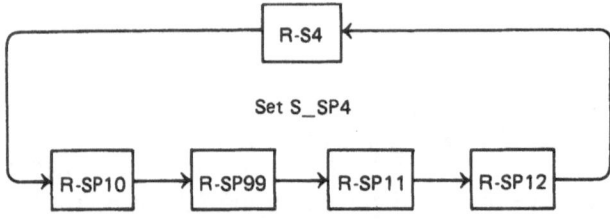

Figure 7.3b   An example of ORDER PRIOR.

DEFAULT

If the order option is DEFAULT, then the order is implementor-defined.

SORTED

If the order option is SORTED, then the member record occurrences in every set of the set type will be maintained in an order based on the sort control key of each member record type defined in a member clause. For example, in Figure 7.1, it is assumed that set type S_SP is 'SORTED' and the member record type SP has a sort control key PNO. The sort control key will be explained in more detail in the paragraph concerning the key clause in Section 7.3.3.

If RECORD TYPE { record-name }... is specified (following the keyword SORTED) with two or more record names, then the set type has two or more member record types and the sequence of record names serves as a sort control key. For example, Figure 7.4 shows a fragment of a University registration database. The occurrences of record types COURSEWORK and EXAM are the records of the academic performance of students in their coursework and examination respectively.

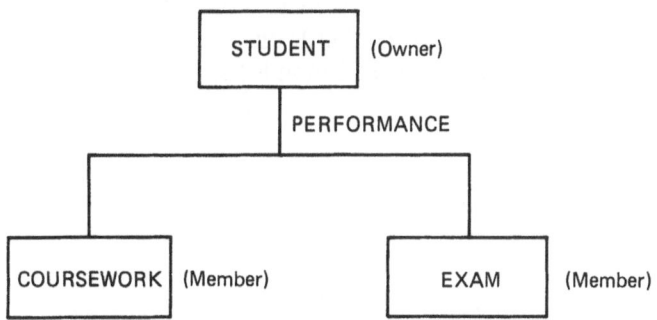

Figure 7.4   An example set type called PERFORMANCE.

The following schema description indicates that all COURSEWORK records will precede the EXAM records in each set type PERFORMANCE.

```
SET  PERFORMANCE
   OWNER  STUDENT
   ORDER  SORTED  RECORD  TYPE  COURSEWORK  EXAM
   .
   .
   .
```

The ordering among those COURSEWORK records and EXAM records will be explained under the paragraph concerning the key clause in Section 7.3.3.

The alternative DUPLICATES specifies the action taken by the database control system when an incoming member record occurrence to be inserted has a key value which is the same as an existing member record occurrence. The rules are as follows:

(a) If PROHIBITED is specified, then the order clause is violated.

(b) If FIRST is specified, then the incoming occurrence will be stored prior to the existing occurrence. If LAST is specified, then the incoming occurrence will be stored next to the existing occurrence.

(c) If DEFAULT is specified, then the ordering will be implementor-defined.

7.3.3 Member Clause

A member clause specifes a member record type of a set type.It consists of six clauses: the member record name clause, the insertion clause, the retention clause, the member uniqueness clause, the key clause, and the member check clause. (See also their format specified in the set type definition.)

Member record name clause

A member record name clause specifies the record name of a member record type of a set type. The record name specified must designate a record type already defined in the containing schema (see also the OWNER clause in Section 7.3.1), and should be unique. The following schema description is therefore prohibited:

```
SET S_SP
   OWNER S
   MEMBER SP

   .
   .
   .

   MEMBER SP
   .
   .
   .
```

Insertion clause

An insertion clause defines the insertion characteristics of a member record type of a set type. There are three insertion modes: AUTOMATIC, MANUAL and STRUCTURAL.

If AUTOMATIC is specified for a member record type of a set type, then each record occurrence of that member record type becomes a member of some set of the set type when the record occurrence is initially stored in the database. The owner record occurrence of the set is identified by the application. For example, let us refer to Figure 7.5 which shows a fragment of a University registration database. The occurrences of record types DEPT and STUDENT are academic department records and student records respectively.

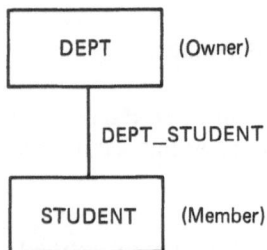

DEPT   (Owner)

DEPT_STUDENT

STUDENT   (Member)

Figure 7.5   An example set type called DEPT_STUDENT

If the University regulations are such that every student must belong to one department only, then the insertion mode of the set DEPT_STUDENT should be AUTOMATIC.

If MANUAL is specified for a member record type of a set type, then records will be inserted as member records in its set by an explicit CONNECT statement (which is a DML statement explained in Section 10.3.5). The owner record occurrence of the set is identified by the application program. For example, suppose the University registration database has a record type called HOSTEL, the occurrences of which are records of the University hostels. The fragment of the database shown in Figure 7.5 can then be represented as shown in Figure 7.6.

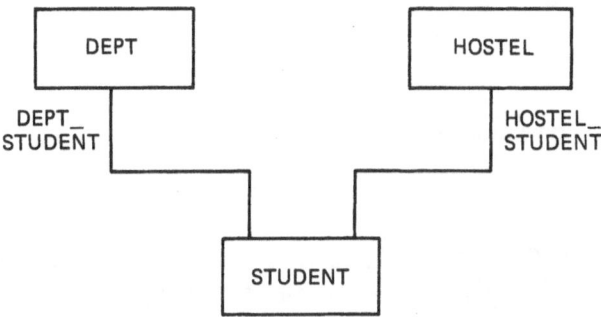

Figure 7.6   Two example set types called DEPT_STUDENT and HOSTEL_STUDENT.

Of course, every student may be free to live in a University hostel or a private flat. If a student lives in a hostel, however, his record will be connected to a record of his HOSTEL. In this case, the insertion mode of the set HOSTEL_STUDENT should be MANUAL.

If STRUCTURAL is specified for a member record type of a set type, then each record occurrence of a member record type becomes a member of some set of that set type when it is initially stored in the database. The owner record is selected by the database management system to have values of specified data items equal to those of the record to be inserted. The format of the structural specification is

```
{   member-component-identifier = owner-component-
    identifier
 |  owner-component-identifier = member-component-
    identifier
}
[{ AND {   member-component-identifier = owner-
           component-identifier
        |  owner-component-identifier = member-
           component-identifier
       }
 }...
]
```

where the owner component identifier and member component identifier both
have the format

```
{   [{ record-name | OWNER | MEMBER }.] component-name
    [subscripts]
  | component-name [subscripts] [ OF {record-name |
    OWNER | MEMBER}]
}
```

For example, consider the set types S_SP of the Suppliers-and-Parts database.
In every set occurrence, the supplier number SNO in the owner record must be
the same as that in every member record. So we can write

```
SET S_SP
  OWNER S
  ORDER ... (details omitted)
  MEMBER SP
    INSERTION STRUCTURAL SP.SNO = S.SNO
```

In the above example 'SP.SNO = S.SNO' is called a component identifier
match, in which SP and S are called qualifiers. They must be specified since the
owner and member record types have the same component name in the match,
namely SNO.

In an NDL database, a set type may have the same record type as both the owner
record type and a member record type. Such a set type is called a 'recursive set
type', which has occurrences called 'recursive sets'. For example, Figure 7.7
illustrates an example of a recursive set, since an officer-in-charge is also
regarded as an employee. If STRUCTURAL is specified in a recursive set type,
OWNER or MEMBER must be specified for every component name.

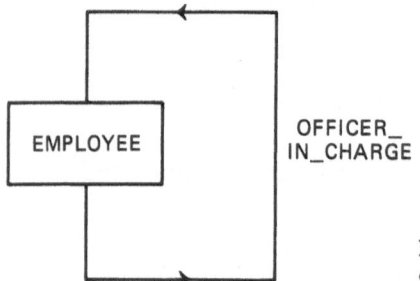

Figure 7.7   An example of a recursive set type
called OFFICER_IN_CHARGE.

Retention clause

A retention clause defines the retention characteristics of a member record type
of a set type.

If FIXED is specified, then a record, having once become a member record of some set, remains a member of that set until it is erased from the database. For example, in the fragment of the University registration database described in Figure 7.5, if there is a regulation stating that a student cannot transfer from one department to another, then set type DEPT_STUDENT should have the retention mode FIXED.

If MANDATORY is specified, then a record, having once become a member record of a set, remains a member of some set of the same set type until it is erased from the database. For example, if it is a University regulation that, under certain circumstances, a student may transfer from one department to another, then set type DEPT_STUDENT should have the retention mode MANDATORY. (Note that a student must however belong to only one department.)

If OPTIONAL is specified, then a record, having once become a member record of some set, need not remain a member of that set or of any set of that set type. For example, in the fragment of the University registration database shown in Figure 7.6, the retention mode of the set type HOSTEL_STUDENT may be optional, since a student can, of course, remain in the University even if he/she has withdrawn from a University hostel.

Member uniqueness clause

A member uniqueness clause specifes a uniqueness constraint for member records of each occurrence of a set type. For example, if every student is assigned a distinct project code in his/her academic department denoted by component name PROJ_CODE (see record type STUDENT in Figure 7.5), we can write

```
UNIQUE PROJ_CODE OF STUDENT
```

Note that, in this example, different departments may use the same set of project codes for students. However, as far as individual departments (i.e owners of set occurrences) are concerned, project codes are distinct.

Key clause

A key clause defines the sort control key for a member record type of a sorted set type. The key clause should be specified only when SORTED is specified in the order clause of the containing set type.

If SORTED RECORD TYPE { record-name }... is specified in the order clause of the containing set type, then RECORD TYPE should be specified once only in the key clause of every member record type. The key item(s) contained in the key clause will be used as key(s) to order the records in the member record type. For example, suppose the record type COURSEWORK in Figure 7.4 has key item CW_CODE (coursework code) and the record type EXAM has key item EXAM_SUB (examination subject) and SUB_LEVEL (subject level). Consider the following schema description (which includes those relevant parts only):

```
SET PERFORMANCE
   OWNER STUDENT
   ORDER SORTED RECORD TYPE COURSEWORK EXAM
   MEMBER COURSEWORK

      .

      .

      .

   KEY ASCENDING CW_CODE
                  RECORD TYPE
   DUPLICATES PROHIBITED

      .

      .

      .

MEMBER EXAM

      .

      .

      .

   KEY ASCENDING EXAM_SUB SUB_LEVEL
                  RECORD TYPE
   DUPLICATES PROHIBITED

      .

      .

      .
```

The schema indicates that in each set of PERFORMANCE, all COURSEWORK records will precede the EXAM records. Moreover, the COURSEWORK records will be sorted by the key item CW_CODE and the EXAM records by EXAM_SUB and SUB_LEVEL.

If SORTED DUPLICATES (instead of SORTED RECORD TYPE {record-name}..) is specified in the order clause of the containing set type, then RECORD TYPE must not be specified in any key clause of the member record type. In this case, each member clause must contain the same number of common key items, which are then used as a sort control key for the ordering of the records of the member record types in a set. The example above will not work in this case since COURSEWORK and EXAM do not have the same number of common key items. To enable it to work, let us change the key item of COURSEWORK to CW_SUB and C_SUB_LEVEL (coursework subject and its level) such that the data types of CW_SUB and C_SUB_LEVEL are identical to that of EXAM_SUB and SUB_LEVEL respectively. Consider the following statements (extracts from a schema description):

```
SET PERFORMANCE
   OWNER STUDENT
   ORDER SORTED DUPLICATES PROHIBITED
   MEMBER COURSEWORK

        .
        .
        .
   KEY ASCENDING CW_SUB C_SUB_LEVEL
        .
        .
        .
   MEMBER EXAM
        .
        .
        .
   KEY ASCENDING EXAM_SUB SUB_LEVEL
        .
        .
        .
```

This schema indicates that in each set of PERFORMANCE, all COURSEWORK and EXAM records will be sorted by 'subject and level'. Note that all the key clauses must specify the same direction for the sorting of keys, which is either ASCENDING or DESCENDING.

From the above two examples, it can be seen that the DUPLICATES clause can be specified either in the ORDER clause or within each of the MEMBER clauses.

Member check clause

A member check clause specifies a validity condition on member records of each occurrence of a set type. The expression of a condition can be very complicated and is explained separately in Appendix B. Syntax and general rules on the member check clause can be found in the ISO document [ISO, 1987b].

7.4 Example Schema of Suppliers-and-Parts

A complete schema description of the Suppliers-and-Parts database is given in the ISO document, which gives a very good demonstration of the use of the data definition language in NDL. This is as follows:

```
SCHEMA SUPPLIERS_AND_PARTS

RECORD S
    UNIQUE SNO
    ITEM SNO        CHARACTER    5
    ITEM SNAME      CHARACTER   20
    ITEM SSTATUS    NUMERIC      3
    ITEM CITY       CHARACTER   15

RECORD P
    UNIQUE PNO
    ITEM PNO        CHARACTER    6
    ITEM PNAME      CHARACTER   20
    ITEM COLOUR     CHARACTER    6
    ITEM WEIGHT     NUMERIC      3 DEFAULT -1
    ITEM CITY       CHARACTER   15

RECORD SP
    UNIQUE SNO PNO
    ITEM SNO        CHARACTER    5
    ITEM PNO        CHARACTER    6
    ITEM QTY        NUMERIC      5
    CHECK QTY >= 0

SET S_SP
    OWNER S
    ORDER SORTED DUPLICATES PROHIBITED
    MEMBER SP
        INSERTION STRUCTURAL SP.SNO = S.SNO
        RETENTION FIXED
        KEY ASCENDING PNO

SET P_SP
    OWNER P
    ORDER SORTED DUPLICATES PROHIBITED
    MEMBER SP
        INSERTION STRUCTURAL SP.PNO = P.PNO
        RETENTION FIXED
        KEY ASCENDING SNO
```

8 Subschema Definition in NDL

8.1 Subschema Definition Language

The subschema is the logical description of that section of the database which is relevant and available to an application. A subschema can, of course, be common to two or more different applications.

The definition of a subschema comprises: (a) a subschema name as well as the name of the schema from which it is derived, (b) one or more record types (otherwise referred to as record views), and (c) one or more set types (otherwise referred to as set views). The term 'view' is appropriate here since it corresponds to that portion of the database the user sees or has available for processing using data manipulation commands.

The NDL syntax allows the Database Administrator (DBA) to choose those record types from the schema which are relevant to a subschema (i.e an application) and rename these if necessary. The DBA may also select from each record type in the schema only those data items (otherwise referred to as component views) which are relevant to a subschema, and rename these accordingly. Set types may also be renamed. The way a subschema is defined using the subschema definition language is clarified below.

A subschema is defined using the format

```
SUBSCHEMA {   schema-name.subschema-name
            | subschema-name OF schema-name
          }
[ { RECORD [ record-name RENAMED ] record-view-name
    [  { ITEM [ component-name RENAMED ] component-
         view-name }...
    | ALL
  ]
  | SET [ set-name RENAMED ] set-view-name
}...
]
```

A subschema defines a user view of the database. The schema name designates a schema, which is called the subject schema of the subschema. The subschema names should be distinct in a subject schema. From the format above, we see that a subschema has two optional descriptive parts, which are called the record view and the set view.

Record view

A record view specifies that a record type is to be included in a subschema, and declares an identifier (which denotes the record view name in the format above) that must designate the record type within the subschema.

A record type in a schema can be renamed and included in a subschema using the option [record-name RENAMED]. The new name is the record view name. If this option is omitted, then the record type is included in the subschema with the same record name specified in the schema.In both cases, the record type in the schema is called the subject record type.

A component name (i.e the name of a data item or array of data items) in the subject record type can also be renamed and included in a subschema by using the option [component-name RENAMED]. Its new name is called a component view name. If ALL is specified instead then all the component names of the subject record type will be included in the subschema with the same names specified in the schema. Examples will be given in the section on the set view below.

Set view

A set view specifies that a set type is to be included in a subschema, and declares an identifier (called a set view name) that must designate the set type within the subschema.

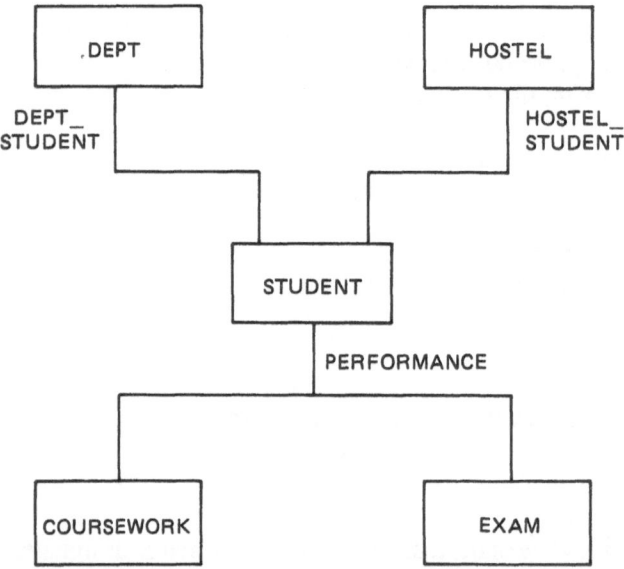

Figure 8.1   A fragment of the University registration database.

A set name in a schema can be renamed and included in a subschema using the option [set-name RENAMED]. The new name is called a set view name. If this option is omitted, then the set type is included in the subschema with the same set name as specified in the schema.

To demonstrate the use of a subschema definition language, consider the combination of Figure 7.4 and Figure 7.6, which results in another fragment of the University registration database as presented in Figure 8.1.

Suppose part of the non-confidential information concerning the students of the University must be released to the students' union. Information regarding each department and examination results are regarded as confidential, with the exception of the department names and addresses. The student's particulars, including identity number, name and home address may be released. Details about University hostel and coursework are not regarded as confidential (assuming that it is the practice of the University that coursework results are always published on the notice board). We can then define a subschema, called UNION_INF, of the schema REGISTRATION of the University registration database as follows:

```
SUBSCHEMA REGISTRATION.UNION_INF
RECORD DEPT
  ITEM DEPT_NAME RENAMED WHAT_STUDY
  ITEM ADDRESS
RECORD HOSTEL
  ALL
RECORD STUDENT RENAMED SCHOOL_MATES
  ITEM ID
  ITEM NAME
  ITEM HOME_ADDRESS RENAMED MAIL_ADDRESS
RECORD COURSEWORK
  ALL
SET DEPT_STUDENT RENAMED WHERE_BELONG
SET HOSTEL_STUDENT RENAMED IN_CAMPUS
SET PERFORMANCE RENAMED ASSIGNMENT_RESULT
```

Of course, for obvious reasons, the students' union should only be allowed to retrieve data from the database through subschema REGISTRATION.UNION_INF and should not have the privilege of update. This can be done by using the READY statement in the procedure of the module concerned, and is explained in Sections 10.2.3 and 10.3.2.

9 Module Language in NDL

9.1 Tasks of the Module Language

The tasks of the module language in NDL are, in principle, the same as those of the module language in SQL discussed in Section 4.1. However, while a procedure in SQL consists of exactly one SQL statement, a procedure in NDL can consist of one or more NDL statements.

9.2 Module Definition and Procedure Definition

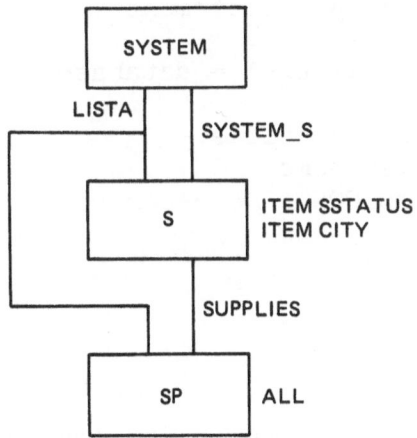

Figure 9.1   An example subschema.

Modules and procedures are defined using the following format:

```
MODULE [module-name]
LANGUAGE { COBOL | FORTRAN | PASCAL | PLI }
SUBSCHEMA {   schema-name.subschema-name
              | subschema-name OF schema-name
            }
[ { SET set-view-name }... ]
{ PROCEDURE procedure-name
  [ {   parameter-name
        {   CHARACTER [length]
          | {   FIXED precision [scale]
              | NUMERIC precision [scale]
              | INTEGER
            }
          | { FLOAT integer | REAL | DOUBLE PRECISION }
        }
        [ OCCURS { unsigned-integer }... ]
    | RECORD
    | STATUS
    | TEST
    }...
  ]
  [ {   commit statement | connect statement
      | disconnect statement
      | erase statement | find statement
      | get statement
      | modify statement | nullify cursor statement
      | ready statement
      | reconnect statement | rollback statement
      | store statement
      | {   TEST database-key-identifier-1 = database-
            key-identifier-2
          | TEST NULL database-key-identifier
          | TEST SET EMPTY set-view-name
          | TEST SET set-view-name CONTAINS database-
            key-identifier
        }
    }...
  ]
}...
```

A module has an optional module name, which is an identifier and should be different from any other module name in the same implementor-defined environment. The LANGUAGE clause specifies the language of the program which   calls the procedure of the module. The schema and subschema names specified following SUBSCHEMA should designate a schema and a subschema respectively in the same implementor-defined environment of the module. The subschema designated is called the subject subschema. The records and sets that can be referenced by the module are defined by the subject subschema.

The option [{ SET set-view-name }...] is called temporary set specification, in which the set view names specified should be distinct. Moreover, each set view name should be different from any set view name specified in the definition of the subject subschema. We will demonstrate the syntax rule of this specification by means of an example. Suppose a temporary set specification is written as follows:

```
SET SV
```

Then the system will define the temporary set type SV in the subschema as:

```
SET SV
    OWNER SYSTEM
    ORDER LAST
```

If there is a record view name called RV, say, specified in the subject subschema, the temporary set specification will define a member clause as follows:

```
MEMBER RV
    INSERTION MANUAL
    RETENTION OPTIONAL
```

An illustrative example to demonstrate the use of the NDL module language is given below [ISO, 1987b] where the subject subschema SUPPLIERS is derived from the schema SUPPLIERS_AND_PARTS (see Section 7.4).

```
SUBSCHEMA SUPPLIERS OF SUPPLIERS_AND_PARTS
RECORD S
    ITEM SSTATUS
    ITEM CITY
RECORD SP
    ALL
SET S_SP RENAMED SUPPLIES
```

An NDL module utilising the subschema SUPPLIERS_AND_PARTS can now be written as follows:

```
MODULE
    LANGUAGE COBOL
    SUBSCHEMA SUPPLIERS OF SUPPLIERS_AND_PARTS
    SET LISTA
    .
    .
    .    (The procedures are specified here;
    .    examples of these are presented later.)
    .
    .
```

In the above example, besides the sets in LISTA, only the records and sets in the subschema SUPPLIERS can be referenced by the module. The description SET LISTA means

```
SET LISTA
   OWNER SYSTEM
   ORDER LAST
MEMBER S
   INSERTION MANUAL
   RETENTION OPTIONAL
MEMBER SP
   INSERTION MANUAL
   RETENTION OPTIONAL
```

Therefore, the database referenced by the module can be depicted as shown in Figure 9.1 (assuming that the set type SYSTEM_S shown in this figure has already been defined).

PROCEDURE

A module can have one or more procedures. Each procedure has a distinct procedure name in the module and contains one or more NDL statements. Parameter names declared in a procedure are distinct and every parameter name contained in the NDL statements must have already been declared, specifying its data type. If a component view name of the subject subschema used in an NDL statement is identical to a parameter name specified in the containing procedure, then its record view name should also be specified, and thus its format becomes

```
record-view-name.component-view-name [subscripts]
```

or

```
component-view-name [subscripts] OF record-view-name
```

The data type definition format for the parameters in a procedure is determined by the language of the program associated with the module which calls the procedure. In the ISO standard, the LANGUAGE clause can specify COBOL, FORTRAN, Pascal or PL/I and the data types to be specified for the parameter procedures are summarised in Table 9.1.

In a procedure, the parameters RECORD, STATUS and TEST can each be specified once, defining a single occurrence of a character string with a length of 30, 5 and 1 respectively. These parameters, if specified, will return useful information to users after the execution of an NDL statement in the procedure, which is summarised as follows:

Case (i): No deadlock occurs in the execution

Parameter	Value of parameter
STATUS	Set to "00000" (which means 'procedure: success').
RECORD	(a) If the database key of the session cursor is not null, it is set to the record view name that designates the record type of the record referenced by that database key. (b) If it is null, it is set to all space characters.

Case (ii): Deadlock occurs in the execution

Parameter	Value of parameter
STATUS	Set to the status code.
TEST	Set to "0".

In case (ii) above, all changes made to the database and session state by the execution of the procedure will be cancelled.

The parameter TEST should be specified if and only if the procedure contains a test statement. A procedure should contain one test statement at most; its use is explained later.

We will use an example of a procedure as follows:

```
PROCEDURE  'find-first-s'
           S_CITY CHARACTER 15
           STATUS
     FIND FIRST S WHERE CITY = S_CITY
```

In this example, the procedure name is 'find-first-s', which should be different from any other procedure name in the containing module. In this procedure, the data item S_CITY is defined to be of data type CHARACTER with length 15.The parameter STATUS is also specified, the use of which was explained previously. The procedure has one NDL statement, that is, FIND.

Table 9.1

Language specified	Data type of parameter name in parameter declaration
COBOL	CHARACTER or NUMERIC
FORTRAN	CHARACTER, INTEGER, REAL or DOUBLE PRECISION
Pascal	CHARACTER, INTEGER or REAL
PL/I	CHARACTER, FIXED or FLOAT

9.3 Using an Embedded NDL Module

In this section, an example of an NDL module is used to illustrate how NDL statements can be embedded in an application program. Consider the following module called SUP_CITY which is defined according to the format specified in Section 9.2:

```
MODULE SUP_CITY
    LANGUAGE COBOL
    SUBSCHEMA SUPPLIERS OF SUPPLIERS_AND_PARTS

    PROCEDURE 'start' STATUS
        READY S SHARED UPDATE

    PROCEDURE 'find-first-s'
            S_CITY CHARACTER 15
            STATUS
        FIND FIRST S WHERE CITY = S_CITY
```

In this module, the clause LANGUAGE COBOL indicates that the host programming language is COBOL. The subschema specified is SUPPLIERS, as detailed in Section 9.2. The module has two procedures, namely, 'start' and 'find-first-s', which are explained in Sections 10.3.2 and 9.2 respectively.

A COBOL host program can be associated with at most one NDL module. The COBOL statement CALL can then be used to execute the DML statements specified in the procedures of the associated NDL module. The corresponding COBOL variables must, of course, be declared within the host program. In the example module SUP_CITY we can include the following data description entries in the data division of a COBOL host program:

```
    .
    .
    .
01  DB-STATUS PIC X(5).
01  S-CITY    PIC X(15).
    .
    .
    .
```

It can be seen that the COBOL data type specifications of DB-STATUS and S-CITY are equivalent to the NDL data type specifications of STATUS and

S_CITY respectively. The parameter STATUS defines a single occurrence of a character string of length 5.

After the COBOL variables DB-STATUS and S-CITY have been declared, a CALL statement can be written in the procedure division of the associated COBOL host program to execute the DML statements of the procedures in the NDL module. This is demonstrated by Examples 1 and 2 below.

Example 1.

```
       .
       .
       .
       CALL 'start' USING DB-STATUS.
       .
       .
       .
```

This statement will prepare record type S for processing by appending the record name S, the share specification SHARED, and the access intent UPDATE, to the ready list of the session state (see Sections 10.2, 10.2.3 and 10.3.2). After the procedure 'start' has been executed, the value of the NDL parameter STATUS will be returned in the COBOL variable DB-STATUS. This value can, of course, be used to check the database status after the call in the COBOL host program.

Example 2.

```
       .
       .
       .
       MOVE 'LONDON' TO S-CITY.
       CALL 'find-first-s' USING S-CITY DB-STATUS.
       .
       .
       .
```

These two COBOL statements select the first record occurrence of record type S with CITY = 'LONDON'. After control has been returned to the COBOL host program, the value of DB-STATUS can, of course, be used to check the database status.

To understand further the way NDL statements can be interfaced with high level programming languages, we present exactly the same module and search logic as before in Pascal.

The Pascal module

```
MODULE SUP_CITY
    LANGUAGE PASCAL
    SUBSCHEMA SUPPLIERS OF SUPPLIERS_AND_PARTS

    PROCEDURE start STATUS
        READY S SHARED UPDATE

    PROCEDURE find_first_s
            S_CITY CHARACTER 15
            STATUS
        FIND FIRST S WHERE CITY = S_CITY
```

Declaration of variables in Pascal

```
        .
        .
        .
var
    DB-STATUS:  string(5);
    S-CITY:     string(15);
        .
        .
        .
```

Calling the Pascal procedure

Example 1.

```
    .
    .
    .
begin
        .
        .
        .
    start(DBSTATUS);
        .
        .
        .
end;
```

Example 2.

```
.
.
.
begin
     .
     .
     .
     SCITY := 'LONDON';
     find_first_s(SCITY, DBSTATUS);
     .
     .
     .
end;
```

10 Data Manipulation in NDL

10.1 Tasks of the Data Manipulation Language

The network data manipulation language (NDL-DML) is used for simple record storage and retrieval with an NDL database. Every procedure in a module contains NDL statements which are executed when the procedure is called by the application program associated with the module. NDL is, of course, interfaced to ordinary high-level programming languages (e.g FORTRAN, Pascal) and allows further analyses and manipulation of data item values.

In an NDL database, data items and records are logically represented as simple hierarchies (trees) using the SET clause.In each set type there is an owner record type and zero, one, or more member record types. By having a member record type in one set type as the owner of another set type we can build complex structures resembling networks and hence a Network Database Language (NDL). All record types, data items, and set types are defined within the logical schema using the schema DDL and are subsequently utilised by appropriate NDL-DML commands.

Throughout this chapter, all examples of DML statements, unless otherwise stated, are written under the assumption that they are statements written in a procedure of a module of which the subschema is defined as

```
SUBSCHEMA SAMPLE OF SUPPLIERS_AND_PARTS
RECORD S
   ALL
RECORD P
   ALL
RECORD SP
   ALL
SET S_SP
SET P_SP
```

where schema SUPPLIERS_AND_PARTS is defined in Section 7.4. The data in the sample Suppliers-and-Parts database given in Appendix D will also be used in the demonstration.

10.2 Session and Session State

Before we study the NDL statements in detail, it is necessary to understand the concept of a session and a session state in NDL database. A database operation is the execution of an NDL statement. A session is the sequence of database operations peformed during the execution of an application program associated with a module.

A session state is an ephemeral object associated with a session. It is created prior to the first database operation in a session and is destroyed after the last database operation in the session. It consists of 'cursors', 'temporary sets' and a 'ready list' (which are quoted here because they are regarded as syntactic constructs in the ISO standard). The session state is available to an application only through NDL statements. The contents of the session state are modified by the DBMS upon execution of NDL statements in a procedure of its associated module.

10.2.1 Cursors

A cursor type can consist of a session cursor, a record cursor and a set cursor, jointly referred to as 'cursors' using the format

```
session-cursor
[record-cursor]...
[set-cursor]...
```

A session cursor is used to identify the current session record (i.e the most recently accessed record, whether it is of the owner or member record type). It has the format

```
{ database-key }
```

which is an implementor-defined value that either identifies exactly one record in the database or is null and identifies no record. (Intuitively, we may think of a database key as the value of a pointer, which is used to model a cursor.)

A record cursor is used to identify the current record of each subschema record type. It has the format

```
{ record-view-name } { database-key }
```

where the database key identifies the record occurrence of the record type.

A set cursor is used to identify the owner record occurrence and the current member record occurrence in the current set of each subschema set type. It has the format

```
{ set-view-name }
{ database-key }
{ position }
```

where the database key and position identify the owner record occurrence and current member record occurrence respectively, and the position may contain one or two database keys. (See also Example 4 in Section 10.3.3 regarding the find specification.)

An 'initial cursors' for a module is a 'cursors' which has the following properties:

(a) The session cursor contains a database key that is *null*.

(b) Every record cursor contains a database key that is *null*.

(c) The database key which identifies the owner record occurrence in the set cursor is *null*, and the position consists of one database key that is *null*.

10.2.2 Temporary Sets

A temporary set type is defined by a temporary set specification. (Recall that temporary set specifications are defined in a module; see Section 9.2.) 'Temporary sets' are used to maintain the contents of all the temporary sets defined by the associated module. Each entry has the format

```
[temporary-set]...
```

where a temporary set is an occurrence of a temporary set type. Initially, the temporary set area contains an empty occurrence for each of the temporary set types.

10.2.3 Ready List

A ready list maintains the ready specifications for each record type that has been activated by a READY statement. It has the format

```
{ empty | { ready-specification }...}
```

An initial 'ready list' is *empty*. The format of a ready specification is given in the description of the READY statement in Section 10.3.2.

10.3 DML Statements and their Classification

10.3.1 Handling of Transactions

COMMIT statement

Format:

```
COMMIT [FINISH]
```

This statement terminates the current transaction and makes permanent all the changes carried out. All changes made to the database by the transaction are made accessible to concurrent sessions. For each temporary set, every member record is removed from membership in that set. The 'cursors' is set to the 'initial cursors' for the subject subschema. If FINISH is specified, then the ready list is set to *empty*.

ROLLBACK statement

Format:

```
ROLLBACK [FINISH]
```

This statement terminates the current transaction with rollback. The effect on the database of all statements executed by the session during that transaction is cancelled. The 'cursors' is set to the 'initial cursors' for the subject subschema. For each temporary set, every member record is removed from membership in that set. If FINISH is specified, then the ready list is set to *empty*.

10.3.2 Readying of Record Types for Processing

READY statement

Format:

```
READY { record-view-name
        { EXCLUSIVE | PROTECTED | SHARED }
        { RETRIEVE | UPDATE }
      }...
```

This statement prepares one or more record types for processing. The specifications shown following READY are called ready specifications, which will be appended to the ready list of the session state if there is no lock conflict. For example, in the module that utilises the subschema SUPPLIERS shown in

Section 9.2, we can define a procedure called 'start' with parameter STATUS as follows:

```
PROCEDURE 'start' STATUS
   READY S SHARED UPDATE
```

It is obvious that to avoid lock conflict, record view name S must not be specified as PROTECTED in any other ready list of a concurrent session state. Table 10.1 on p.106 shows a complete list of those situations which will cause lock conflict. Note that the above example of a lock conflict pertains to case (c) in Table 10.1.

10.3.3 Location of Record Occurrences

FIND statement

Format:

```
FIND { {   SESSION | record-view-name
       | { OWNER | MEMBER } set-view-name
     }
    |{   FIRST | LAST | NEXT | PRIOR
       | { ABSOLUTE | RELATIVE } signed-integer
     }
     {   record-view-name
       | [ record-view-name ] IN set-view-name
       | SUBSCHEMA RECORD
     }
     [ WHERE condition ]
   }
   [ FOR { RETRIEVE | UPDATE } ]
   [   RETAIN ALL
    | { [ AS MEMBER { set-view-name }...]
        [ RETAIN RECORD
          | RETAIN SET { set-view-name }...
          | RETAIN RECORD SET { set-view-name }...
        ]
      }
   ]
```

From the above format, we see that the FIND statement has one compulsory part and two optional parts, and these are called 'find specification', 'find intent', and 'find cursor disposition' respectively.

Table 10.1

Ready specification in a session state	Ready specification in a concurrent session state
(a) S EXCLUSIVE	S specified
(b) S specified	S EXCLUSIVE
(c) S SHARED UPDATE	S PROTECTED
(d) S PROTECTED UPDATE	S PROTECTED or S UPDATE
(e) S PROTECTED RETRIEVE	S UPDATE

Find specification

The format of the find specification shows that there are two ways of locating a specific record occurrence in the database. The first is to locate a record using

```
{ SESSION | record-view-name | { OWNER | MEMBER }
  set-view-name }
```

which is called a 'database key identifier' and references a database key. Its use will be demonstrated by Examples 1 to 4 below. Another way to locate a record occurrence is to use what is called a search specification. This is explained in Examples 5 to 10 below. In all examples 1 to 10 the object subschema is SAMPLE, as explained in Section 10.1.

Example 1. FIND SESSION

The database key of the most recently accessed record, irrespective of whether it is an owner or a member record type, is used to locate that record.

Example 2. FIND S

The database key contained in the record cursor for the record type S is used to locate the record occurrence in the database.

Example 3. FIND OWNER S_SP

The owner database key contained in the set cursor for the set type S_SP is used to locate the record occurrence in the database.

Example 4. FIND MEMBER S_SP

The position contained in the set cursor (see the format of set cursor) for S_SP will be used for the location of the record occurrence. There are two possibilities here. If the position consists of a single database key, then this key will be used. If the position consists of a pair of database keys, then the database key for location will be set to *null* and no record will be located. The message 'find: database key is null' will also be sent by the DBMS.

The alternative for locating a specific record occurrence in the database is called a search specification which consists of three parts as shown in the format of the find specification. The first two parts are compulsory, and specify the search orientation (FIRST, LAST, etc) and the domain of the search specification (record view name, etc). The domain is a group of record occurrences from which one is to be selected. The third part is an optional WHERE condition. (The format of a condition is given in Appendix B.) This alternative for locating a record occurrence will be explained in Examples 5 to 10 below.

Example 5. FIND FIRST P WHERE CITY = "LONDON"

In this example, the domain of the search specification consists of all record occurrences of the record type P and the first record occurrence of P with CITY = "LONDON" will be selected. Referring to the example database described in Appendix D, the occurrence with part number P1 will be selected.

Example 6. FIND RELATIVE 2 P WHERE CITY = "LONDON"

Following the FIND statement in Example 5, this statement will locate the second record occurrence in P with CITY = "LONDON", hence the record occurrence with part number P6 will be selected. (If the number 2 in this example is changed to say, 3, then the message 'find: no record found' will be sent by the DBMS.)

Example 7. FIND PRIOR P WHERE CITY = "LONDON"

Following the FIND statement in Example 6, this statement will locate the record occurrence in P with part number P4.

Example 8. FIND FIRST IN S_SP

In this example, the first member record occurrence of the set referenced by the owner database key of the set cursor for S_SP will be selected. For example, let us refer to the pictorial representation of S_SP in Figure 7.1. If the current set is S_SP2, then the record occurrence selected will be R-SP7.

Example 9. FIND FIRST S IN LISTA

It is assumed that this FIND statement is written in a procedure of the module that utilises the subschema SUPPLIERS described in Section 9.2. The set type LISTA has two member record types (see also Section 9.2). Record type S is specified in the FIND statement, so the record occurrences of record type SP will not be included in the domain of the search specification in the statement. As a result, the first record occurrence of S in the current set of LISTA will be selected.

In this example, LISTA has SYSTEM as its owner record type (i.e it is a 'singular set type'). It also has a unique set which is called a 'singular set'. So, the record occurrence of S with supplier number S1 will be selected.

Example 10. FIND FIRST SUBSCHEMA RECORD

In this example, the domain of the search specification consists of all record occurrences of the record types in the subschema under consideration, namely, subschema SAMPLE (see Section 10.1). The ordering of the record occurrences in the domain is implementor-defined.

Throughout Examples 1 to 10 above, providing no database errors arise, the database key of the session cursor will then be set to the respective selected record.

Find intent

The find intent, as shown in the FIND statement, has the format

```
FOR { RETRIEVE | UPDATE }
```

So, if Example 8 above is re-written as

```
FIND FIRST S IN LISTA FOR UPDATE
```

then the record occurrences in S can be updated (using the CONNECT statement, DISCONNECT statement, etc) provided S has been specified in a READY statement for UPDATE. If find intent is not specified, then it is assumed to be FOR RETRIEVE. Of course, a database error will arise if RETRIEVE is specified in the READY statement and the find intent specifies an UPDATE.

Find cursor disposition

The last part in the FIND statement is the find cursor disposition. It is an option to update the database keys of the owner and member record occurrences in the set cursor.

If the find cursor disposition is omitted or it does not specify ALL or RECORD, then the database key of the record cursor designated by the record view name of the selected record is set to the database key of the selected record.

If the find cursor disposition is omitted or it does not specify ALL, then each set cursor whose set view name is not specified following the keywords RETAIN SET or the keywords RETAIN RECORD SET is updated in accordance with the following cases:

(a) If the record type of the selected record is the owner record type of the set type of the set cursor, and if the set view name that designates the set cursor is not specified following the keywords AS MEMBER, then the owner data-base key of that set cursor is set to the database key of the selected record, and the position of that set cursor is set to *null*.

(b) If the selected record is a member of a set occurrence of the set type desig-
     nated by the set view name of the set cursor, proceed as follows: If either the
     record type of the selected record is not the owner record type of that set type
     or the set view name of the set cursor is specified following the keywords AS
     MEMBER, then
     (1) The position of the set cursor is set to the database key of the selected
     record.
     (2) If that set type is a non-singular set type, then the owner database key of
     the set cursor is set to the database key of the owner record occurrence of that
     set occurrence.

The set cursor should not be updated, except in cases (a) and (b) above. Finally,
if the set view name of the set cursor is specified following the keywords AS
MEMBER, then the selected record should be a member of some set occurrence
of the set type designated by that set view name, otherwise a database error will
arise.

10.3.4 Manipulation of Record Occurrences

ERASE statement

Format:

```
ERASE  {   SESSION  |  record-view-name
          |  { OWNER  |  MEMBER } set-view-name
       }
  WITH { FULL CASCADE | PARTIAL CASCADE }
```

This statement removes one or more records from the database. For example,

```
ERASE SP WITH FULL CASCADE
```

In this example, the object database key is the database key contained in the
record cursor for the record type SP. (Of course, this database key should not be
null and SP should be included in the ready list for UPDATE, otherwise a
database error will arise.) Suppose the record cursor is (see also Section 10.2.1)

```
SP  K-SP11
```

where K-SP11 is the database key which identifies record R-SP11 in Figure 7.1.
Then the ERASE statement will result in the following remove operation (see also
Appendix C)

```
K-SP11
S_SP
```

since record R-SP11 is a member of a set of S_SP. Record R-SP11 is called the object record of this ERASE statement. In general, the remove operation will be performed for each set type of which the object record is currently a member. In the Suppliers-and-Parts database, since R-SP11 is also a member record of set type P_SP, the remove operation

```
K-SP11
P_SP
```

will also be performed.

The specification 'WITH FULL CASCADE' in this example has no effect on the erasure since SP is not the owner record type of any set type. More records will be affected, however, if the object record is an owner record. For example,

```
ERASE S WITH FULL CASCADE
```

In this example, since S is an owner record type of a set type, in addition to those necessary remove operations to be performed as mentioned in the example above, there are affected sets and affected records. The affected sets are those whose owner record is the object record, and the affected records are those that are members of one or more affected sets.

Suppose the database key contained in the record cursor for S is K-S4, which identifies record R-S4 in Figure 7.1. In this example, the affected set is S_SP4 and the affected records are R-SP10, R-SP11 and R-SP12. The specification 'WITH FULL CASCADE' will result in the erasure of all the affected records.

The use of the specification 'WITH PARTIAL CASCADE' cannot be demon-strated using the Suppliers-and-Parts database; however, we list the rules of this specification as follows:

(i)   The affected set should not contain any mandatory member, otherwise a data base error will arise.

(ii) Any affected record that is a fixed member of any affected set will be erased.

(iii) For each affected record that is an optional member of any affected set, the remove operation will be performed, in which the database key and the set name (or set view name) will be that of the affected record and the affected set respectively.

Finally, cursors will also be updated as a result of the ERASE statement. If the database key of the session cursor or any record cursor is equal to the database key of the object record, then it is set to *null*. If the owner database key in any set cursor is equal to the database key of the object record, then the owner database key and the position of that set cursor are set to *null*.

GET statement

Format:

```
GET record-view-name
   { SET parameter-name [subscripts] TO operand }...
```

This statement sets parameter values to component values from a selected record occurrence. The record view name designates a record cursor containing a database key which identifies the object record to be 'got'. A database error will arise if this database key is *null*. For example,

```
GET S SET S_NAME TO SNAME SET S_STATUS TO SSTATUS
      SET S_CITY TO CITY
```

The clause {SET ... TO ...} is called 'to parameter move clause'. There are three such clauses in this example. Suppose data is transferred successfully from the 'source operand' SNAME to the 'target identifier' S_NAME in the first clause, but a database error arises on the data transfer from SSTATUS to S_STATUS in the second. Then the effect of the first clause will be retained and the rest of the clauses will not be performed. However, the database key of the session cursor will be set to that of the object record.

In general, the data transfer performed in a 'to parameter move clause' has the following rules:

(i)   The data type of the source operand should be the same as that of the target identifier, except that the former can be exact numeric or approximate numeric when the latter is approximate numeric.

(ii) Both the source operand and target identifier should be a data item or array. The data item referenced by the target identifier is called a target item.

(iii) If the literal delivered by the operand is a character string, its length should be less than or equal to that of the target item, otherwise a database error might arise. The examples in Table 10.2 demonstrate some special cases of data transfer. Each pair of numerals in brackets in the left hand column shows the lengths of the character strings of the literal delivered by the source operand and the target item respectively, and a space is denoted by 'b'.

If the data type of the target item is exact numeric, then the numeric literal delivered by the source operand should be representable in exactly the same way as a literal of the target item data type, otherwise a database error will arise. For example, if the data type of the target item is FIXED 3 2, it cannot accommodate a numeric literal such as +1234.567 delivered by the source operand.

If the data type of the target item is approximate numeric, then the target item is set to the numeric literal delivered by the source operand.

Table 10.2

Lengths	Literal delivered by source operand	Target item set to
(4,4)	ABCD	ABCD
(6,4)	ABCDb	ABCD
(6,4)	ABCDEF	(Database error arises)
(2,4)	AB	ABbb

MODIFY statement

Format:

```
MODIFY record-view-name
    [ SET { [ record-view-name.] component-view-name
              [subscripts]
            | component-view-name [subscripts] [ OF
              record-view-name]
         }
      TO operand
    ]...
```

This statement replaces the contents of one or more data items in a record occurrence. The record view name specified immediately after the keyword MODIFY is called the object record view name. It should be currently included in the ready list for update, otherwise a database error will arise. The object record view name designates a record cursor, of which the database key must not be *null*. The object record is the record identified by this database key.

The option [SET ... TO ...] in the format above is called 'to database move clause'. In each of these clauses, the operand is evaluated, and data transfer is performed. Rules on data transfer in a 'to database move clause' are the same as those of the 'to parameter move clause' detailed in the section on the GET statement. A MODIFY statement can usually be accomplished simply by data transfer, with the exception of two cases exemplified by Examples 1 and 2 below.

Example 1. MODIFY SP SET SNO TO NEW_SNO

Here, the literal delivered by NEW_SNO is "S3". The assumption we make here is that the retention clause of the member record type SP under the set type S_SP does not specify FIXED in the schema defined in Section 7.4. The reason for this assumption is given below.

In the above example, the object record type is SP, and the object record is to be determined by the record cursor. Let us refer to set S_SP4 in Figure 7.1, which is redrawn in Figure 10.1 with the record keys shown. Suppose the database key of the record cursor is K-SP11, identifying record R-SP11. R-SP11 then becomes the object record.

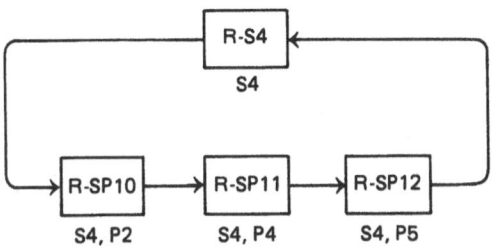

Figure 10.1   An occurrence of set type S_SP based on set S_SP4 of Figure 7.1 with record keys shown.

After the data transfer is performed, the value "S4" for SNO in record R-SP11 is replaced by "S3". The MODIFY statement cannot be accomplished simply in this way, however, because the insertion clause of the member clause of SP under set type S_SP is STRUCTURAL, and SNO appears as a member component identifier in the insertion clause (see the schema in Section 7.4 and insertion clause in Section 7.3.3). The following steps must therefore be carried out in order to accomplish the statement in this case:

(a) Perform the remove operation (see also Appendix C)

```
K-SP11
S_SP
```

(b) Perform the insert operation (see also Appendix C)

```
K-SP11
S_SP
D
retain
```

where D is the database key which identifies the record occurrence of record type S (the owner record type of S_SP) in which the value for S.SNO is equal to "S3". (In this example, the record occurrence turns out to be R-S3 as shown in Figure 7.1 and Appendix D.) Of course, a database error will arise if there is no such match.

The contents of sets S_SP3 and S_SP4 after the above steps have been performed are presented in Figure 10.2 and Figure 10.3 respectively.

In fact, if we do not make the assumption that the retention clause of the member record type does not specify FIXED, then a database error will arise since the retention clause of SP under S_SP specifies FIXED and the set occurrence S_SP3 into which the object record R-SP11 was inserted is not the set occurrence S_SP4. We wish to point out that in order to demonstrate how the MODIFY

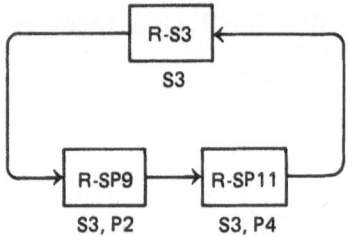

Figure 10.2   Set S_SP3 after the completion of manipulative operations.

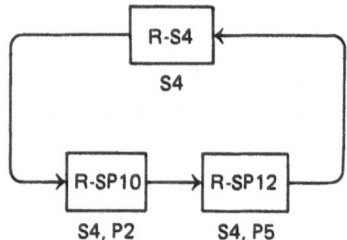

Figure 10.3   Set S_SP4 after the completion of manipulative operations.

statement works when STRUCTURAL insertion clauses are involved, we must assume that the retention clause of member record type SP in set type S_SP does not specify FIXED in the schema. Moreover, the object record type SP in the above MODIFY statement is a member of both set types S_SP and P_SP, hence the above steps should also be carried out for set type P_SP.

Example 2. MODIFY SP SET PNO TO NEW_PNO

This MODIFY statement cannot be accomplished simply by data transfer since PNO appears in the key clause of SP under set type S_SP. (Note that PNO also appears in the insertion clause of SP under set type P_SP which specifies STRUCTURAL; this creates the same problem as that explained in Example 1 above.) Again, supposing the object record is R-SP11 as shown in Figure 10.1, the following steps must be carried out after the data transfer:

(a) Perform the remove operation

```
K-SP11
S_SP
```

(b) Perform the insert operation

```
K-SP11
S_SP
D
retain
```

where D is the database key of the owner record occurrence of the set from which R-SP11 is removed. In this example, the owner record occurrence is R-S4. The aim of steps (a) and (b) above is to arrange the key PNO in the appropriate order as specified in the schema. If the object set type is singular, with SYSTEM as the owner record type, then *null* will be used for the owner database key in the insert operation.

Note that Example 1 has the same problem as Example 2 since SNO in Example 1 also appears in the key clause of SP under set type P_SP. This problem, however, may be solved in the same way.

The execution of the MODIFY statement should not of course cause any violation to any record uniqueness clause, member uniqueness clause, key clause, order clause, record check clause or member check clause, otherwise a database error will arise. We conclude our description of the MODIFY statement with another example.

Example 3. MODIFY S SET CITY TO P.CITY CURSOR

In this example, the option CURSOR in the operand becomes compulsory, which means that the database key of the record cursor for record type P will be used to identify the source record in P, in order that the value of the data item designated by CITY in that record can be evaluated.

STORE statement

Format:

```
STORE record-view-name
   [ SET {   [record-view-name.] component-view-name
             [subscripts]
           | component-view-name [subscripts] [OF
             record-view-name]
         }
     TO operand
   ]...
   [   RETAIN ALL
     | RETAIN RECORD
     | RETAIN SET { set-view-name }...
     | RETAIN RECORD SET { set-view-name }...
   ]
```

This statement stores a record in the database. The record view name specified immediately after the keyword STORE is called the object view name, which designates the object record type. The object view name should of course be currently included in the ready list for update, otherwise a database error will arise. The first option in the format is the 'to database move clause', which was described previously under the MODIFY statement. The second option in the format is called 'store retention'.

The general rules of the STORE statement are very complicated. We will demonstrate how it works using examples based on a simple schema called DEMONSTRATION described below. We will also present the rules which apply to more complex cases when necessary.

```
SCHEMA DEMONSTRATION
RECORD DEPT
UNIQUE DEPT_CODE
ITEM DEPT_CODE     CHARACTER 2
ITEM DEPT_NAME     CHARACTER 10

RECORD STUDENT
UNIQUE ID
ITEM ID            CHARACTER 7
ITEM NAME          CHARACTER 25
ITEM SUBJECT       CHARACTER 10
ITEM ADDRESS       CHARACTER 50 DEFAULT "NA"

RECORD RESULT
UNIQUE EXAM_NO
ITEM EXAM_NO       CHARACTER 3
ITEM GRADES        CHARACTER 20

SET DEPT_STUDENT
   OWNER DEPT
   ORDER SORTED DUPLICATES PROHIBITED
   MEMBER STUDENT
      INSERTION AUTOMATIC
      RETENTION MANDATORY
      KEY ASCENDING ID

SET STUDENT_RESULT
   OWNER STUDENT
   ORDER SORTED DUPLICATES PROHIBITED
   MEMBER RESULT
      INSERTION AUTOMATIC
      RETENTION FIXED
      KEY ASCENDING EXAM_NO
```

The following statements define a subschema called AMEND which is used as the basis for implementing subsequent data manipulation examples:

```
SUBSCHEMA AMEND OF DEMONSTRATION
RECORD DEPT
    ALL
RECORD STUDENT
    ALL
RECORD RESULT
    ALL
SET DEPT_STUDENT
SET STUDENT_RESULT
```

Consider the following STORE statement, written in a procedure of a module of which the subschema is AMEND:

```
STORE STUDENT SET ID TO "8600001"
              SET NAME TO "SMITH JOHN"
              SET SUBJECT TO "COMPUTING"
              RETAIN SET DEPT_STUDENT
```

where the set type DEPT_STUDENT has a current set. Let Ki be the database key of the owner record of this set. We will describe briefly the steps required to perform the above STORE statement.

(a) Create a record occurrence of type STUDENT in the database. The new record occurrence is the object record. Denote its implementor-defined database key by Kj.

(b) Perform the data transfer. This means that ID is set to "8600001", NAME is set to "SMITH JOHN", etc. (For further details see the 'to database move clause' in the section concerning the MODIFY statement.)

(c) Establish the object record as the owner of an empty set for set type STUDENT_RESULT.

(d) Perform the insert operation:

```
Kj
DEPT_STUDENT
Ki
retain
```

In a more complex case, however, the object record in step (c) should be established as the owner of an empty set for any set type in which the object record type is the owner record type. Also, step (d) should be carried out for all set types for which the object record type is a member record type with AUTOMATIC specified in the insertion clause (e.g MEMBER STUDENT in SET DEPT_STUDENT described in schema DEMONSTRATION). Moreover, the set cursor disposition in step (d) in the example is *retain* because set type DEPT_STUDENT is specified in the store retention of the example STORE statement; otherwise it should be *update*. If RETAIN ALL is specified in the example, the set cursor disposition should again be *retain*. Finally, note that item ADDRESS in STUDENT is not assigned any value in the example. No database error would arise provided this item has a default value specified in the schema, as in this example.

In order to demonstrate another case of how a STORE statement is performed, let us change the insertion clause of MEMBER STUDENT in set DEPT_STUDENT in schema DEMONSTRATION from

```
INSERTION AUTOMATIC
```

to

```
INSERTION STRUCTURAL STUDENT.SUBJECT = DEPT.DEPT_NAME
```

In this case, the description above for the example STORE statement still applies, with the exception that step (d) should be amended as follows:

(d) Perform the insert operation

```
Kj
DEPT_STUDENT
K
retain
```

where K is the database key which identifies the occurrence of record type DEPT (the owner record type of DEPT_STUDENT) in which the value for DEPT_NAME is equal to "COMPUTING". A database error will of course arise if there is no such match.

As a result of the STORE statement, generally, the session cursor will be set to reference the object record.

With regard to the function of the store retention on a record cursor and set cursor, if neither ALL nor RECORD is specified, then the record cursor for the record view name will be set to reference the object record (i.e the newly created record occurrence; see step (a) of the STORE statement above). If the store retention does not specify ALL, then for each set type described in the subject subschema in which the object record type is the owner record type, its set cursor will be updated provided it is not included in the store retention. For example, in subschema AMEND above, we find set type STUDENT_RESULT which has the object record type STUDENT as the owner record type. Moreover, STUDENT_RESULT is not included in the store retention in the example. The set cursor for STUDENT_RESULT will then be updated. The method for updating is to set the owner database key of the set cursor to the database key of the object record and set the position of the set cursor to *null*. So, in our example, the set cursor for STUDENT_RESULT is updated to

```
STUDENT_RESULT
Kj
null
```

Finally, in order to avoid a database error, a STORE statement should not cause any violation in the record uniqueness clause and record check clause.

10.3.5 Connection Between Records and Set Occurrences

CONNECT statement

Format:

```
CONNECT {  SESSION | record-view-name
         | { OWNER | MEMBER } set-view-name
         }
     TO set-view-name
```

This statement establishes the membership of a record occurrence in a set. The compulsory part following the keyword CONNECT is a database key identifier, which references a database key (see find specification in FIND statement) called an object database key. If SESSION or { OWNER I MEMBER } set-view-name is specified, then the object record type is the record type referenced by the object database key. If record view name is specified, then the name will reference the object record type. Let us refer to the set type HOSTEL_STUDENT described in Section 7.3.3 and depicted in Figure 7.6. Suppose we write

```
CONNECT STUDENT TO HOSTEL_STUDENT
```

then the object record type is STUDENT. This CONNECT statement will work provided STUDENT is a member record type of HOSTEL_STUDENT, and has an insertion clause specifying MANUAL or a retention clause specifying OPTIONAL in the set type HOSTEL_STUDENT; otherwise a database error will arise. STUDENT should, however, be currently included in the ready list for update. Finally, the following insert operation will be performed as a result of the above CONNECT statement:

```
Kj
HOSTEL_STUDENT
Ki
update
```

where Kj is the database key in the record cursor for STUDENT (in general, we should say 'the object database key'), which should not be *null*. Ki is the owner database key of the set cursor for HOSTEL_STUDENT.

DISCONNECT statement

Format:

```
DISCONNECT {  SESSION | record-view-name
           | { OWNER | MEMBER } set-view-name
           }
      FROM set-view-name
```

This statement removes a record from set membership in a specified set type. The description on the database key identifier and the set view name following the keyword FROM has already been given in the section on the CONNECT statement and will not be repeated here. This statement is in fact the reverse of the CONNECT statement and so we give an example similar to the one given in the CONNECT statement above:

```
DISCONNECT STUDENT FROM HOSTEL_STUDENT
```

In this example, the statement will work provided STUDENT is a member record type of HOSTEL_STUDENT, and has a retention clause specifying OPTIONAL in the set type HOSTEL_STUDENT. Moreover, STUDENT should be currently included in the ready list for UPDATE. Finally, the following remove operation will be performed as a result of the above DISCONNECT statement:

```
Kj
HOSTEL_STUDENT
```

where Kj is the database key in the record cursor for STUDENT (i.e the object database key), which should not be *null*.

RECONNECT statement

Format:

```
RECONNECT {  SESSION | record-view-name
          | { OWNER | MEMBER } set-view-name
          }
      IN set-view-name
```

This statement changes the membership of a record occurrence in a set type. The description of the database key identifier and the set view name following the keyword IN has already been given in the section on the CONNECT statement. Consider an example similar to that given in the CONNECT statement:

```
RECONNECT STUDENT IN HOSTEL_STUDENT
```

In this example, the statement will work provided STUDENT is a member record type of HOSTEL_STUDENT. Of course, STUDENT should be currently included in the ready list for UPDATE. The two steps to accomplish the RECONNECT statement above are as follows:

(a) Perform the remove operation

```
Kj
HOSTEL_STUDENT
```

where Kj is the database key in the record cursor for STUDENT (i.e the object database key), which should not be *null*.

(b) Perform the insert operation

```
Kj
HOSTEL_STUDENT
Ki
update
```

where Ki is the owner database key of the set cursor for HOSTEL_STUDENT.

In step (b) above, if STUDENT has a retention clause specifying FIXED in HOSTEL_STUDENT, then the set into which the object record is to be inserted should be the set from which it was removed. Otherwise a database error will arise.

10.3.6 Nullifying Cursors

NULLIFY cursor statement

Format:

```
NULLIFY {   SESSION | record-view-name
          | { OWNER | MEMBER } set-view-name
        }
```

This statement sets the referenced cursor to *null*. The database key identifier specified in the format references a database key (see the find specification under the FIND statement in Section 10.3.3). As a result of this statement, the database key referenced will be set to *null*. For example, as a result of the statement

```
NULLIFY S
```

the database key contained in the record cursor (see Section 10.2.1) for the record type S will be set to *null*.

10.3.7 Test for Database Key, Set and Set Membership

Test database key equal statement

Format:

```
TEST operand1 = operand2
```

This statement determines whether two database keys reference the same record. If the database keys referenced by operand1 and operand2 reference the same record occurrence, then the value of the TEST parameter is set to "1"; otherwise it is set to "0". A database error will arise if the database key referenced by operand1 or operand2 is *null*. Consider the example

```
TEST SESSION = S
```

Here, if the database key contained in the record cursor (see Section 10.2.1) for record type S is the same as the database key of the most recently accessed record, then the value of the TEST parameter will be set to "1". Otherwise it will be set to "0".

Test database key null statement

Format:

```
TEST NULL {   SESSION | record-view-name
            | { OWNER | MEMBER } set-view-name
          }
```

This statement determines whether a database key is *null*. The database key identifier (specified following the keyword NULL) references a database key (see the find specification under the FIND statement in Section 10.3.3). If this database key is *null*, the value of the TEST parameter will be set to "1"; otherwise the value of the TEST parameter will be set to "0". For example, the statement

```
TEST NULL S
```

will test whether the database key contained in the record cursor (see Section 10.2.1) for record type S is *null* or not.

Test set empty statement

Format:

```
TEST SET EMPTY set-view-name
```

This statement determines whether a set has any member records. The set type designated by the set view name specified is called the object set type. The object set cursor is the set cursor designated by the set view name.

If the object set type is singular, then the object set is the singular occurrence of the object set type.

If the object set type is non-singular, then the object set is the set referenced by the object set cursor. (The owner database key of the set cursor should not be *null*, otherwise a database error will arise.)

The value of the TEST parameter will be set to "0" if the object set has one or more members whose record type is included in the subject subschema; otherwise it will be set to "1". (The subject subschema is the subschema of the containing module of the procedure in which this test statement is written.) Consider the example

```
TEST SET EMPTY S_SP
```

Here, the object set cursor (see Section 10.2.1) is the set cursor designated by set type S_SP. The statement will test whether the current set of record type S_SP has any member records or not.

Test set membership statement

Format:

```
TEST SET set-view-name
    CONTAINS {   SESSION | record-view-name
             | { OWNER | MEMBER } set-view-name
             }
```

This statement determines whether a record is a member of some occurrence of a set type. The database key identifier (specified following the keyword CONTAINS) references a database key (see the find specification under the FIND statement), which is called the object database key. The object database key should not be *null*, and the record type of the record that it references should be defined as a member record type of the set type designated by the set view name (which is specified following the keyword SET in the format); otherwise a database error will arise in either case. For example, in the statement

```
TEST SET S_SP CONTAINS SP
```

the object database key is the database key of the record cursor for SP, and it should not be *null*. Also, SP is a member record type of S_SP. In this example, if the record referenced by the object database key is a member of an occurrence of the set type S_SP then the value of the TEST parameter is set to "1"; otherwise it is set to "0".

Appendix A.   Values, Search Conditions and Queries in SQL

In this appendix we describe 'value expression', 'search condition' and 'query expression' in SQL. These three terms are dealt with separately so as to leave the format of those SQL-DDL and SQL-DML statements in earlier chapters more compact and user-friendly. Value expression, search condition and query expression can have very complicated recursive expressions and their respective specifications are expressed in Backus-Naur Form (BNF) here. Examples are also given to demonstrate their special features.

Value Expression

Format in BNF *(see over)* :

```
value-expression::=
  term
  | [+|-] term + value-expression

term::=
    factor
  | term * factor
  | term / factor

factor::=
  [+|-] primary

primary::=
    value-specification
  | column-specification
  | set-function-specification
  | (value-expression)

value-specification::=
    parameter-specification
  | variable-specification
  | literal
  | USER

parameter-specification::=
  parameter-name [indicator-parameter]

indicator-parameter::=
  [INDICATOR] parameter-name

variable-specification::=
  embedded-variable-name [indicator-variable]

indicator-variable::=
  [INDICATOR] embedded-variable-name

column-specification::=
  [table-name. | correlation-name. ] column-name

set-function-specification::=
  COUNT(*) | distinct-set-function | all-set-function

distinct-set-function::=
  { AVG | MAX | MIN | SUM | COUNT }
      (DISTINCT [table-name. | correlation-name.]
      column-name)

all-set-function::=
  { AVG | MAX | MIN | SUM } ([ALL] value-expression)
```

From the above specification, we see that a value expression can be written in a very complicated form. Let us consider some examples for demonstration purposes. The value expression

```
SALARY * 1.2 + MAX(FRINGE)
```

is of the form 'term * factor + value expression', since a term, a factor and a value expression can be a column name, a literal and a set function specification respectively. A more compact way of expressing this would be to say that it is a 'term + value expression', since a term can mean term * factor. Furthermore, the value expression

```
(SALARY * 1.2 + MAX(FRINGE) ) / YR_OF_SERVICE
```

is of the form term/factor, since a term can be a primary of the format '(value-expression)', and so we can say that the value expression example above is a 'term'.

The value specification and set function specification specified above require further clarification.

Value specification

Value specification specifies one or more values or parameters. The optional indicator parameter has data type exact numeric with a scale of 0. The value specified by the parameter specification is null when the value of the indicator parameter is negative, otherwise it is the value of the parameter identified by the parameter name. (See also the FETCH statement in Section 5.2.2.) The value specified by USER is set to the module authorization identifier of the module which contains the SQL statement whose execution caused the USER value specification to be evaluated. The variable specification [ISO, 1987a] is used in an embedded SQL application program.

Set function specification

Set function specification specifies a value derived by the application of a function to an argument. The argument of COUNT(*), the argument source of a distinct set function, or the argument source of an all set function is a table (or a subset of a grouped table) specifed by the FROM clause of the table expression. For example, in

```
SELECT COUNT(*)
FROM EMPLOYEE
```

the argument of COUNT(*), which is a set function specification, is the table EMPLOYEE. In the example

```
SELECT MAX(SALARY + FRINGE)
FROM EMPLOYEE
```

the argument source of the all set function MAX(SALARY + FRINGE) is the table EMPLOYEE, and the argument of MAX is the value expression SALARY + FRINGE (with the keyword ALL omitted).

The results of a set function specification are listed below, where R denotes the argument or argument source of a set function specification, and S denotes the argument of a distinct set function or an all set function.

Function	Result
COUNT(*)	Cardinality of R
COUNT	Cardinality of S
AVG	Average of values in S
MAX	Maximum value in S
MIN	Minimum value in S
SUM	Sum of values in S

Search Condition

Format in BNF:

```
search-condition::=
  boolean-term | search-condition OR boolean-term

boolean-term::=
  boolean-factor | boolean-term AND boolean-factor

boolean-factor::=
  [NOT] boolean-primary

boolean-primary::=
  predicate | (search-condition)
```

A search condition specifies a condition that is 'true', 'false' or 'unknown', depending on the result of applying boolean operators to specified conditions. From the format shown above, we see that the WHERE clause can consist of a single predicate (which is the most common case) or a series of such predicates linked by the operators AND or OR. The following example demonstrates some of these features:

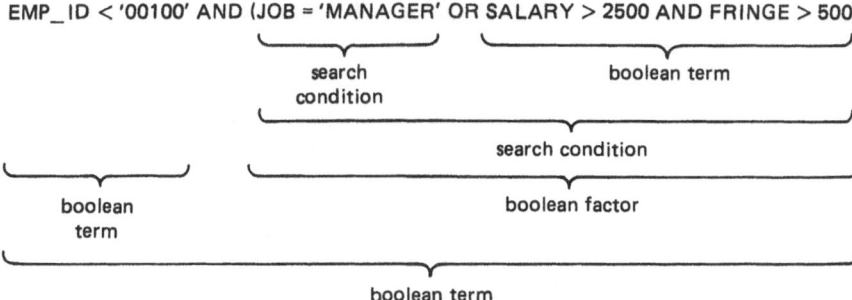

EMP_ID < '00100' AND (JOB = 'MANAGER' OR SALARY > 2500 AND FRINGE > 500)

Query Expression

Format in BNF:

```
query-expression::=
   query-term | query-expression UNION [ALL] query-term

query-term::=
   query-specification | (query-expression)
```

A query expression specifies a query. UNION is the union operator in traditional set theory. If ALL is not specified, then redundant duplicate rows in the result of the UNION will be eliminated. For example, suppose each department has only one manager (referring to the definition of tables EMPLOYEE and MERIT in Section 3.2). The following UNION of tables

```
SELECT DEPT
FROM EMPLOYEE
WHERE JOB = 'MANAGER'
AND SALARY > 3000

UNION

SELECT DEPT
FROM MERIT
WHERE TUNROVER > 1000000
```

will give a list of distinct departments which have either a manager with a salary of over 3,000 or a turnover of over 1,000,000.

Appendix B.   Conditions in NDL

In NDL, a condition specifies an expression that must be evaluated as either *true* or *false*. Its format is best expressed in BNF as follows:

```
condition::=
      alternative [ { OR alternative }... ]

alternative::=
      simple-condition [ { AND simple-condition}... ]

simple-condition::=
      subcondition
    | negated-subcondition
    | relation-condition

subcondition::= (condition)

negated-subcondition::= NOT (condition)

relation-condition::=
      operand  relation  operand

relation::=
      < | <= | = | >= | > | <>
```

As seen in the format of a condition, the expression it specifies can be very complicated. We will demonstrate some explanatory examples using the Suppliers-and-Parts database given in Appendix D.

Example 1

Consider the condition

```
SNAME = "JONES" OR STATUS >= 20
```

It can be analysed as

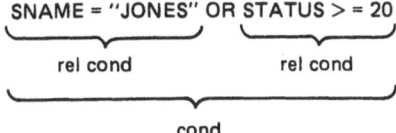

where the words relative and condition are abbreviated as 'rel' and 'cond' respectively.

Suppose we write (see also the subschema SAMPLE of SUPPLIERS_AND_ PARTS in Section 10.1)

```
FIND FIRST S WHERE SNAME = "JONES" OR STATUS >= 20
```

then, as a result of this FIND statement, the record occurrence in S with supplier number "S1" will be located.

Example 2

Consider the analysis of a more complicated condition shown below.

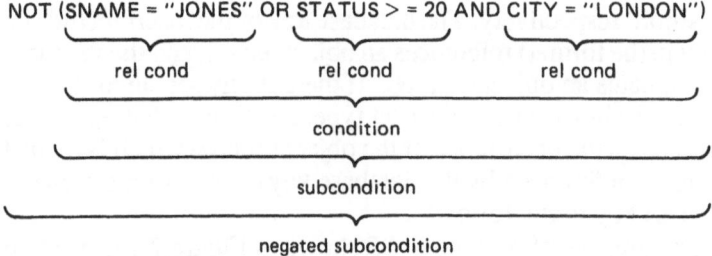

If we write

```
FIND FIRST S WHERE NOT (SNAME = "JONES"
                        OR STATUS >= 20
                        AND CITY = "LONDON")
```

then the record occurrence in S with supplier number "S3" will be located.

Appendix C.   Auxiliary NDL Operations

Two auxiliary operations, namely the insert and the remove, are used in the definition of NDL data manipulation statements in Chapter 10. They will be described in the following two sections.

Insert Operation

Format:

```
{ database-key }
{ set-name | set-view-name }
{ database-key }
{ retain | update }
```

This operation inserts a record occurrence into a set. The four parts in the format above are called 'insert record', 'insert set type', 'insert set owner', and 'insert cursor disposition' respectively. The database key of the insert record (i.e the first database key in the format) references an object record, and the set name or set view name designates an object set type. If there is any set cursor having a set view name which designates the object set type, then it is called the object set cursor. The object set is the occurrence of the object set type which is owned by the record occurrence referenced by the database key of the insert set owner (i.e the second database key in the format).

Referring to the occurrences of set type S_SP shown in Figure 7.1 in Section 7.3.2 as an example, suppose record occurrence R-S2 is identified by database key K-S2 (which is, in fact, an implementor-defined value). Also, suppose that a record occurrence called R-SP0, which is identified by database key K-SP0, in record type SP is to be inserted into set S_SP2. Then, in the insert operation Ins described by

```
K-SP0
S_SP
K-S2
update
```

the object record, object record type, object set and object set type are R-SP0, SP, S_SP2 and S_SP respectively. (The insertion cursor disposition in operation Ins is assumed to be *update*, which will be explained later.)

Using an insert operation, the object record is inserted as a member of the object set in accordance with the set ordering criteria specified by the order clause or the key clauses of the object set type. The cases when the order options are FIRST, LAST, DEFAULT and SORTED are obvious and will not be explained here. If the order clause specifies NEXT or PRIOR, the result of the operation will depend on the position of the object set cursor. We will again use the occurrences of set type S_SP as shown in Figure 7.1 in Section 7.3.2 as an example.

In the example let records R-SP7 and R-SP8 be identified by database keys K-SP7 and K-SP8 respectively. If the object set cursor is

```
S_SP
K-S2
K-SP7
```

then by performing the insert operation Ins above, record R-SP0 will be inserted into set S_SP2. The results for the cases when the order options of set S_SP are NEXT and PRIOR are depicted by Figures C.1 and C.2 respectively.

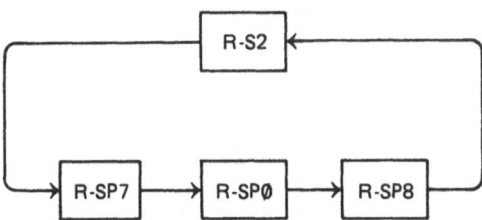

Figure C.1   Set S_SP2 (ORDER NEXT).

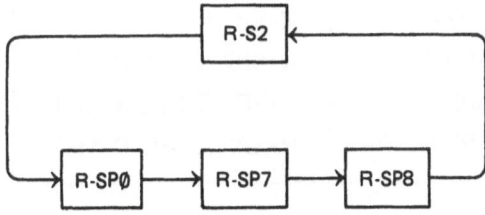

Figure C.2   Set S_SP2 (ORDER PRIOR).

From this example, we see that the result of the insert operation depends on the position of the object set cursor and the order option in the order clause of the object set type. The following table gives a summary of the general rules:

| Position of object set cursor | Place of insertion of object record | |
	ORDER NEXT	ORDER PRIOR
Ki	after Ki	before Ki
null	first in set	last in set
Ki Kj	after Ki	before Kj
Ki *null*	after Ki	last in set
null Ki	first in set	before Ki

where

Ki, Kj	=	database keys which are not *null*
after/before a key	=	as a member record in the object set immediately after/before the member record referenced by a database key K
first/last in set	=	as the first/last member record in the set occurrence referenced by the object set cursor

To demonstrate these general rules, a comprehensive list of the sample results of the insert operation Ins on set S_SP2 is given in the table below. (Note that the cases depicted by Figures C.1 and C.2 are case (a).)

| | | Result | |
Case	Position	ORDER NEXT	ORDER PRIOR
(a)	K-SP7	R-SP7 R-SP0 R-SP8	R-SP0 R-SP7 R-SP8
(b)	*null*	R-SP0 R-SP7 R-SP8	R-SP7 R-SP8 R-SP0
(c)	K-SP7 K-SP8	R-SP7 R-SP0 R-SP8	R-SP7 R-SP0 R-SP8
(d)	K-SP8 *null*	R-SP7 R-SP8 R-SP0	R-SP7 R-SP8 R-SP0
(e)	*null* K-SP7	R-SP0 R-SP7 R-SP8	R-SP0 R-SP7 R-SP8

It is of course assumed that the insert operation would not cause any violation to any member uniqueness clause, order clause and key clause in the object set type, or to any member check clause or implied member check clause derived from the INSERTION clause. Otherwise a database error will arise.

Finally, we come to the last part of the insert operation - the insert cursor disposition. If an object set cursor is present the insert cursor disposition is used to update it. The position of the object set cursor will be set to the database key of the object record if (a) or (b) below is true.

(a) The insert cursor disposition is *update*.

(b) The insert cursor disposition is *retain* and the following condition is true: the position of the object set cursor is a pair of database keys such that either the first such database key references a record that immediately precedes the object record in the object set or the second such database key references a record that immediately follows the object record in the object set.

Remove Operation

Format:

```
{ database-key }
{ set-name | set-view-name }
```

This operation removes a record occurrence from a set. The two parts in the format above are called 'remove record' and 'remove set type' respectively. The database key references an object record, and the set name or set view name designates an object set type. The object set is the occurrence of the object set type of which the object record is a member. Referring to the occurrences of set type S_SP in Figure 7.1 in Section 7.3.2 as an example, suppose record occurrence R-SP11 is identified by database key K-SP11. Then, in the remove operation R described by

```
K-SP11
S_SP
```

the object record, object set type and object set are R-SP11, S_SP and S_SP4 respectively.

With a remove operation, the object record will be removed from the membership of the object set. The relative order of other members of the object set remains unchanged. In the example above, after the remove operation, set S_SP4 can be represented as shown in Figure C.3.

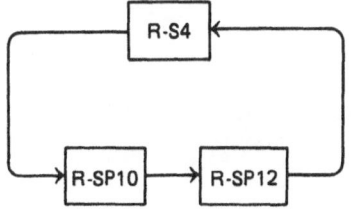

Figure C.3 Set S_SP4 after remove operation R.

If there is any set cursor whose set view name designates the object set type, it will be updated provided (a) its position is a single database key that references the object record, or (b) its position is a pair of database keys, one of which references the object record. The following example demonstrates how the update is carried out.

Let the database keys of record occurrences R-S4, R-SP10 and R-SP12 be K-S4, K-SP10 and K-SP12 respectively. The following table shows how the contents of the set cursor associated with set type S_SP satisfying case (a) or (b) above are updated after the remove operation R is performed.

Set cursor (current)	Updated set cursor
(1) S_SP K-S4 K-SP11	(1) S_SP K-S4 K-SP10 K-SP12
(2) S_SP K-S4 K-SP11 K-SP12	(2) S_SP K-S4 K-SP10 K-SP12
(3) S_SP K-S4 K-SP10 K-SP11	(3) S_SP K-S4 K-SP10 K-SP12

Alternatively, suppose that the remove operation is

```
K-SP10
S_SP
```

then the contents of the set cursor associated with set type S_SP satisfying case (a) or (b) will be as follows

Set cursor (current)	Updated set cursor
(1) S_SP K-S4 K-SP10	(1) S_SP K-S4 *null* K-SP11
(2) S_SP K-S4 K-SP10 K-SP11	(2) S_SP K-S4 *null* K-SP11
(3) S_SP K-S4 *null* K-SP10	(3) S_SP K-S4 *null* K-SP11

Appendix D.   An Example Database
of Suppliers-and-Parts

The example database presented here has been adapted from Date [Date, 1981] and is also used in the ISO report [ISO, 1987b]. A simple example such as this is very appropriate for the illustration of NDL commands. Figure D.1 depicts the structure (model) of the database where S (supplier), P (part) and SP (shipment) are record types.

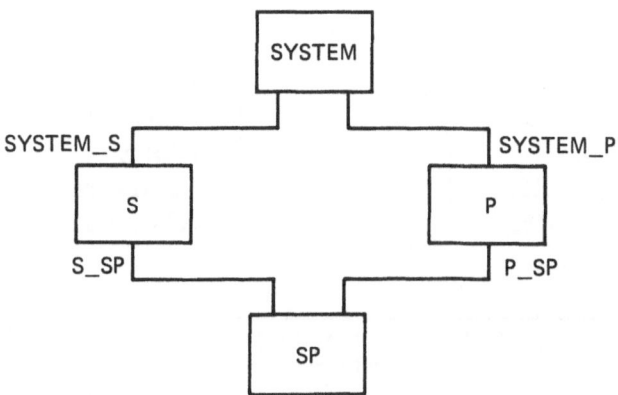

Figure D.1   Structure of Suppliers-and-Parts database.

   S has four data items:

```
SNO         (supplier number)
SNAME       (supplier name)
SSTATUS     (supplier status code)
CITY        (location of supplier)
```

   P has five data items:

```
PNO         (part number)
PNAME       (part name)
COLOUR      (part colour)
WEIGHT      (part weight)
CITY        (location in which the part is stored)
```

   SP has three data items:

```
SNO     (supplier number of shipment)
PNO     (part number of shipment)
QTY     (quantity shipped)
```

Data items in S and P are self-explanatory. In SP, an occurrence implies the shipment of a part (specified by PNO) supplied by a supplier (indicated by SNO) with a given quantity (indicated by QTY).

Each supplier has a unique supplier number and exactly one name, status value (indicated by status code) and location. Each part has a unique part number and exactly a single name, colour, weight and location. Not more than one shipment exists for a given supplier/part combination in SP. The following tables present example occurrences under S, P and SP:

S

SNO	SNAME	SSTATUS	CITY
S1	SMITH	20	LONDON
S2	JONES	10	PARIS
S3	BLAKE	30	PARIS
S4	CLARK	20	LONDON
S5	ADAMS	30	ATHENS

P

PNO	PNAME	COLOUR	WEIGHT	CITY
P1	NUT	RED	12	LONDON
P2	BOLT	GREEN	17	PARIS
P3	SCREW	BLUE	17	ROME
P4	SCREW	RED	14	LONDON
P5	CAM	BLUE	12	PARIS
P6	COG	RED	19	LONDON

SP

SNO	PNO	QTY
S1	P1	300
S1	P2	200
S1	P3	400
S1	P4	200
S1	P5	100
S1	P6	100
S2	P1	300
S2	P2	400
S3	P2	200
S4	P2	200
S4	P4	300
S4	P5	400

Appendix E.   SQL Keywords

ALL	EXISTS	ORDER
AND	FETCH	PASCAL
ANY	FLOAT	PLI
AS	FOR	PRECISION
ASC	FORTRAN	PRIVILEGES
AUTHORIZATION	FOUND	PROCEDURE
AVG	FROM	PUBLIC
BEGIN	GO	REAL
BETWEEN	GOTO	ROLLBACK
BY	GRANT	SCHEMA
CHAR	GROUP	SECTION
CHARACTER	HAVING	SELECT
CHECK	IN	SET
CLOSE	INDICATOR	SMALLINT
COBOL	INSERT	SOME
COMMIT	INT	SQL
CONTINUE	INTEGER	SQLCODE
COUNT	INTO	SQLERROR
CREATE	IS	SUM
CURRENT	LANGUAGE	TABLE
CURSOR	LIKE	TO
DEC	MAX	UNION
DECIMAL	MIN	UNIQUE
DECLARE	MODULE	UPDATE
DELETE	NOT	USER
DESC	NULL	VALUES
DISTINCT	NUMERIC	VIEW
DOUBLE	OF	WHENEVER
END	ON	WHERE
END-EXEC	OPEN	WITH
ESCAPE	OPTION	WORK
EXEC	OR	

Appendix F. NDL Keywords

ABSOLUTE	IN	REAL
ALL	INSERTION	RECONNECT
AND	INTEGER	RECORD
AS	ITEM	RELATIVE
ASCENDING	KEY	RENAMED
AUTOMATIC	LANGUAGE	RETAIN
CASCADE	LAST	RETENTION
CHARACTER	MANDATORY	RETRIEVE
CHECK	MANUAL	ROLLBACK
COBOL	MEMBER	SCHEMA
COMMIT	MODIFY	SESSION
CONNECT	MODULE	SET
CONTAINS	NEXT	SHARED
CURSOR	NOT	SORTED
DEFAULT	NULL	STATUS
DESCENDING	NULLIFY	STORE
DISCONNECT	NUMERIC	STRUCTURAL
DOUBLE	OCCURS	SUBSCHEMA
DUPLICATES	OF	SYSTEM
EMPTY	OPTIONAL	TEST
ERASE	OR	TO
EXCLUSIVE	ORDER	TYPE
FIND	OWNER	UNIQUE
FINISH	PARTIAL	UPDATE
FIRST	PASCAL	WHERE
FIXED	PLI	WITH
FLOAT	PRECISION	
FOR	PRIOR	
FORTRAN	PROCEDURE	
FROM	PROHIBITED	
FULL	PROTECTED	
GET	READY	

References

CODASYL, 'Conference on Data Systems Languages', Report, 1971.

CODASYL, 'Report of the CODASYL Data Description Language Committee', Information Systems, Vol. 3, pp. 247-320, 1978.

Codd, E. F., 'A Relational Model of Data for Large Shared Data Banks', CACM, Vol. 13, No. 6, pp. 377-387, 1970.

Date, C. J., 'An Introduction to Database Systems', Vol. I, Addison-Wesley: (a) Third Edition, 1981, and (b) Fourth Edition, 1986.

Goldfine, A., 'Using the Information Resource Dictionary Command Language', ISO TC97/SC21 N474, 1984.

IBM, 'SQL/Data System Concepts and Facilities', GH24-5013-1, 1982.

IBM, 'DATABASE 2: Introduction to SQL', GC26-4082-0, 1983.

International Organisation for Standardisation (ISO), 'Information Processing Systems - Database Language SQL', ISO 9075, 1987a.

International Organisation for Standardisation (ISO), 'Information Processing Systems - Database Language NDL', ISO 8907, 1987b.

Yannakoudakis, E. J., 'The Architectural Logic of Database Systems', Springer-Verlag, 1988.

Yannakoudakis, E. J. & Cheng, C. P., 'A Rigorous Approach to Data Type Specification', Computer Bulletin, Vol. 3, Part 4, pp. 31-36, 1987.

Subject Index